WAY BEYOND THE IQ

J. P. GUILFORD

Published By
The Creative Education Foundation, Inc.
in association with
Bearly Limited

Printed in the United States of America
Library of Congress Catalog Card Number: 77-80536
ISBN 0-930222-01-6

Bearly Limited joins with the
Creative Education Foundation
in gratefully acknowledging the
efforts of Angelo M. Biondi
in the coordination and production
of this project.

Contents

Foreword

We are delighted to introduce this first in a series of *popular classics* initiated by the Creative Education Foundation on the major research and development thrusts in the study of creativity. It is truly fitting that the series is launched by this special synthesis written by a true astronaut of the human intellect, Dr. J. P. Guilford. He digests herein his quarter century of detailed and unique scholarly efforts in this field.

Because this book is intended for all serious general readers rather than for specialized or technical groups to which his earlier writings were addressed, it might be well to highlight the fact that Dr. Guilford laid the stage for research in creativity in his historic inaugural speech in 1950 as president of the American Psychological Association. In that address he decried the lack of scholarly attention to that most important human phenomenon, creativity. Taking up his own challenge, he embarked on a life-long study of the detailed nature of the human intellect, including its unique creative facets. Now in this book, he brings his major contribution regarding the *Structure of Intellect* to every man, woman, and young adult who is interested in looking "way beyond his or her I. Q."

Dr. Guilford has brought his ideas to countless audiences including the "boundary pushers" who come to our week-long Creative Problem-Solving Institutes from widely diverse fields. People like these, interested in stretching beyond the frontiers of their own creative potential and in helping others do likewise, especially appreciate the challenge of Dr. Guilford's work.

Over the years, Dr. Guilford has contributed specifically to the Creative Education Foundation's goals and achievements in a number of significant ways: as a leader at our Institutes, as a member of our Advisory Board of the *Journal of Creative Behavior,* as a key member of the National Advisory Committee to the Creative Studies Project at State University College at Buffalo, and most recently, as a member of the Foundation's Board of Trustees. As a result of the extensive research project undertaken at our college over a period of years, applying Dr. Guilford's comprehensive *Structure of Intellect,* a series of four experimental courses has now been made a regular part of the college's undergraduate program, and a Master of Science Degree Program in Creative Studies has been established, as well as an Interdisciplinary Center for Creative Studies.

In 1970, Governor Nelson Rockefeller presented Dr. Guilford with the Foundation's "Founder's Medal" in recognition of his contributions, saying:

> I would like to take this opportunity to say what a pleasure it is to participate as Governor in presenting this medal to Dr. Guilford. In my opinion, the importance of creation, of creative education, creative relationships, the whole concept of that quality which human beings have, which is so rare in the world and which is so needed at this period when our society is becoming increasingly mechanistic and people are feeling alienated from government and alienated from society [cannot be overemphasized]. . . . To me this is one of those opportunities when it's a great pleasure to be able to present an award to a man who has evidenced that quality in life which is so important at this particular moment in the history of the world.

Way Beyond the IQ will serve to help many thousands of individuals to study and expand their intellectual capacities. As an additional aid to achieve this goal, an exercise book is currently being developed as a companion piece. It will contain actual practice material for "boundary breakers" who wish to develop the skills that Dr. Guilford has so comprehensively isolated in the pages that follow.

My personal association with Dr. Guilford has spanned a rich 20 years. Like many others, I not only admire his scholarly ability, but also his amazing humility and humaneness.

If you find the contents of this book valuable in your own pursuits and care to tell us about it, we would enjoy hearing from you.

Sidney J. Parnes
Creative Education Foundation
State University College at Buffalo
Buffalo, New York 14222

Preface

If you have ever wished that you, or anyone for whom you have had some responsibility — your child, your pupils or students, or your employees or counselees — were more intelligent or creative, then this book is for you. You will find in these pages numerous guidelines for working toward such goals.

Discoveries during the past quarter century, particularly, have shown the nature of human intellect. That knowledge is the best possible basis for managing our intellectual processes and resources and for promoting development.

Instead of looking at intelligence as one general resource for understanding and problem solving, measurable by a single value, the IQ, or intelligence quotient, we now see that it is composed of a very large number of distinct abilities or functions. Since we know about the various functions and what they are like, we are prepared to do something about them.

Because of many logical interrelationships among the abilities, they have been organized in a single comprehensive system — the author's *Structure-of-Intellect* model. The features of this model provide us with some principles that are of additional value in understanding and controlling mental operations.

In this volume, each ability is liberally illustrated by kinds of tasks in which it is featured, so that the use of concrete examples will aid in understanding what otherwise seems abstract. The reader is usually given a few examples of test items on which he can try his skill of each kind, thus providing an opportunity to make first-hand observations.

Suggestions are frequently given as to roles the abilities play in daily life, as to where and how they may be utilized, and how they may be developed. Considerable attention is given to ways in which skills may be improved in problem solving and creative thinking.

Following some chapters a few optional exercises are provided with which the reader can check his grasp of the book's content. For those who wish to pursue certain subjects further, suggested readings are given.

Acknowledgements and thanks must be offered to many individuals who have facilitated the preparation of this volume. Some chapters in their early forms were read by high-school students, Barry Smith and David Luckeman, with the assistance of Dr. Richard C. Youngs. Sister Katherine Sexton read all the chapters and made numerous helpful suggestions for improvements.

For helping to develop the background information, I am indebted to a great many able and loyal graduate students who worked with me in the Aptitudes Research Project at the University of Southern California over a period of 20 years. In alphabetical order, they are: Raymond M. Berger, Paul A. Bradley, Stephen W. Brown, Paul R. Christensen, Anna B. Cox, Richard de Mille, Jack L. Dunham, James W. Frick, Sheldon F. Gardner, Arthur Gershon, Moana Hendricks, Alfred F. Hertzka, John R. Hills, Ralph Hoepfner, Kaaren I. Hoffman, Norman W. Kettner, Alvin Marks, Philip R. Merrifield, Kazuo Nihira, Maureen O'Sullivan, Hugh Peterson, Mary L. Tenopyr, and Robert C. Wilson. All made significant contributions in furthering knowledge of the nature of intelligence.

For the use of numerous test items I am indebted to the copyright owner, Sheridan Psychological Services, who generously granted permission. Most of the tests were the original brainchildren of the students listed above.

I must thank, also, those from whom I have borrowed some illustrations. They include John E. Arnold, Robert J. Gillespie, Alex F. Osborn, Sidney J. Parnes, and Sidney X. Shore, who over a period of several decades have been active in the Annual Creative Problem-Solving Institutes in Buffalo, New York. I am indebted to Calvin W. Taylor for his help with the title of this volume.

J. P. Guilford

CHAPTER ONE

Intelligence Has Many Components

On the world scene today, by all odds, the name of the game is problem solving. Shortages of materials and threats of even more severe shortages are painfully evident in the face of a population explosion and spreading demands for higher standards of living. Such tensions lead to many frustrations, which can easily erupt into acts of violence, and eventually, wars. On a much smaller scale, personal problems have become more numerous and complex in a rapidly changing world, affording popular newspaper columnists such as Ann Landers or Dear Abby, more work than they can handle.

How are all these problems, large and small, to be solved? Assuming that there is a will to solve them, the answer lies in the most valuable of all our resources, those of the human intellect. Human brains — human intellects — are the most important resources we have to meet this situation.

Although we are often told that our intellectual levels are determined by the genes that we inherit from our ancestors, and that we could do most to improve the intellect by seeing to it that the next generations are well-born in this respect, this choice would be much too slow to meet rapidly increasing needs. Besides, the necessary measures would be mostly beyond our control. On the other hand, it should not be doubted for a moment that intellectual powers of those living today can be expanded by taking appropriate steps. In the words of a song that Bing Crosby used to sing, "You can be better than you are." This proposition applies to our intelligence.

Today we know much better what we have to do in order to improve intelligence because we know considerably more about the *nature* of intelligence. One of the most important steps a person can take toward increasing his own intellectual powers is to know about the kinds of abilities that he has. This fact has been frequently demonstrated in a number of ways.

ABOUT THE IQ

Intelligence tests have been around so long that the IQ (intelligence quotient) associated with them has almost become a household term. IQ tests were invented by Alfred Binet at the beginning of this century, with the purpose of predicting whether individual children should be expected to learn rapidly enough to keep up with children of normal progress. An IQ test does give us an approximation of how well a person will probably learn from reading and listening to verbal instruction. IQ tests have served fairly well for this particular purpose, even though we are aware of the misapplications and misinterpretations that still exist.

Unfortunately, there has been enough success with IQ tests to help foster a false conviction that intelligence is a broad, unitary ability, and that it is best indicated by degree of success in school work. The idea of a single, broad ability was contrary to Binet's own view, for he saw intelligence as a composite of many different abilities. Accordingly, he developed quite a variety of tests that were the basis of his intelligence scale. Even so, we know now that the net result was that only a few of the intellectual abilities were represented by the Binet scale and by other scales that followed it. Not even Binet foresaw the whole range of abilities that were to be found.

In time, intelligence tests were applied in the selection of students for admission to college. They became known more appropriately as "academic-aptitude tests," which would also have been a better name for most intelligence tests. We should be cautioned, however, that tests of the IQ type are far from adequate for predicting achievement in *all* school subjects. For example, in order to meet some other needs, special aptitude tests have been added for selecting students in medicine and law. Furthermore, it is being found that tests of aptitude for college do not accurately predict a person's success after college because success in positions after college depends upon still other abilities and other traits of personality.

For a special example, let us take the case of predicting how well a person will learn to become an airplane pilot. Success in learning to fly a small airplane depends mostly on abilities that are quite different from those measured by IQ tests. For one thing, a student pilot must have a keen appreciation of where he is with reference to his surroundings. He must also be able to imagine what his airplane is doing in space and what he should do next. These talents may not seem like intellectual qualities, but it will be seen in later chapters why they *are* intellectual, when we view intelligence as broadly as we should. Such abilities, for example, are important in higher mathematics.

Incidentally, by determining that these, and other abilities, are important for learning to fly an airplane, and by developing tests to assess them, psychologists in the U. S. Air Force during World War II achieved some remarkable results. At the beginning of the war, the percentage of students who failed in primary pilot training was about 35. Three years later, with selection of students by means of tests for eight abilities, the failure rate dropped to about 10 percent.

SOME EXAMPLES OF TESTS OF DIFFERENT ABILITIES

At this point, let us consider some examples of abilities, most of which are never repesented in IQ tests. For each ability a sample test item will be given. From the sample item, try to see what kind of ability is involved. Think, also, about your degree of strength in that kind of ability.

Example One

In the item of *Figure 1.1,* which person, *A, B, C,* or *D,* shows nearly the same state of mind as the person on the extreme left? You do not need to name the state of mind or describe it; you need only to match two persons who are in a similar state of mind. Of the four alternatives it is person *D* who seems to be quite positive and is trying to make a point, as in an argument or in making a speech.

Figure 1.1

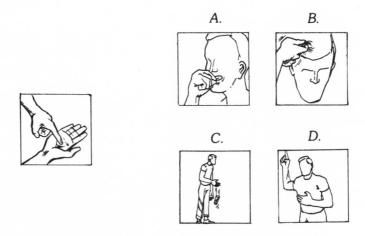

Example Two

In *Figure 1.2,* which object, *A* through *E,* is exactly the same in shape as the block at the extreme left? Each alternative block has a small extension at a particular corner of one side. The correct block is turned in a different position from that of the block at the left. In answer *E* only does the block have the extension in the right place with respect to the total block.

Figure 1.2

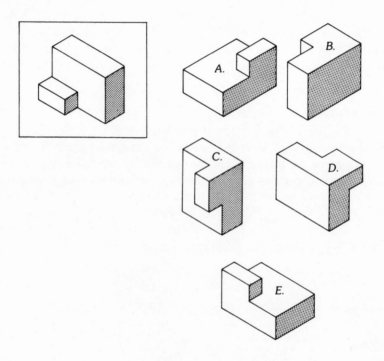

Example Three

The next example makes use of *Figure 1.3.* The three diagrams are different monograms for a person whose initials are *H, E,* and *B.* Give yourself (or a friend) one minute to study the three diagrams then remove them. You (or your friend) should try to sketch the same designs as fully as you can, being careful to present the same arrangements. Reproducing the exact sizes of the letters is not important. You will, of course, easily remember that the letters are *H, E,* and *B.*

Figure 1.3

Example Four

The next task is one of learning to associate a certain number with the name of the football player to whom the number belongs. Here are the paired names and numbers:

Bob Evers   57
Cal Sands   84
Steve Adams 61
John Cole   93
Fred Porter 29

Ask a friend to study this list of pairs for one minute, telling him that he will later be given the names in scrambled order; and that he will be asked to attach each given number to its proper name. The scrambled list is as follows (numbers have also been scrambled):

Steve Adams   29
John Cole   57
Bob Evers   61
Fred Porter   84
Cal Sands   93

Example Five

Figure 1.4 shows two persons, each with a somewhat different facial expression, but the combination of the two offers some basis for interesting personal relations that could occur between the two. Your task is to invent some of the possible relations. Show the nature of those relations by making a list of things the girl is saying to the man in each case. Make as many different relations as you can. The girl might be saying:

> *Dad, I just have to have the car tonight.*
> *I didn't mean it that way.*
> *How can you think that's so funny?*
> *Here I am, just shaking with chills, and you just smile.*

What others do you think of?

Figure 1.4

Example Six

In *Figure 1.5* you see a rather simple, regular design. How many different letters of the alphabet can you see in it? Using the given lines, arranged as they are, make different capital letters, without adding any other lines. You may take liberties with the letters that you make, for example, making letters that normally have curved lines, using only straight lines. The same letter may be made more than once, using different lines. You may use only a part of a line segment, if you wish. Almost all of the letters of the alphabet can be made.

Figure 1.5

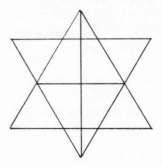

Example Seven

You have undoubtedly had the experience of grouping things in classes, with all the members of each class having at least one thing in common. Your next task is to group some three-letter, nonsense words. Group the following "words" in as many different three-word classes as you can:

DAS   ICO   EUM   AMC   UFI   FZA   PAG   KOE

Also name the feature that is in common to the members of each class. Make your attempt before reading further, in order to observe what you have to do.

Four possible classes are:

DAS   AMC   FZA   PAG   *(Each contains the letter A.)*
ICO   EUM   UFI   KOE   *(Each contains two vowels.)*
DAS   EUM   PAG   KOE   *(Each has a vowel in the middle.)*
ICO   UFI   FZA   KOE   *(Each ends with a vowel.)*

Example Eight

The next test item also deals with classes, but in a different way, and with different kinds of things to be grouped — real objects. Which of the lettered objects is in the same class as the object whose name is in capital letters?

BOMB   A. atom   B. airplane   C. wind   D. cannon
E. fuse

Although most of these things have some connection with a bomb, only D, cannon, is actually also in the same class of *weapons*.

Example Nine

How good are you at drawing sound conclusions from facts that you know? Can you tell whether or not a conclusion is justified by the given facts? Believe it or not, these questions refer to two different abilities. The following item is in the second area:

FACT: *In Buna-Buna in the South Pacific, the game of
ticky-ticky is played outdoors.*

Which of these conclusions is most justified?

A. *People in Buna-Buna like to play games.*
B. *The weather in Buna-Buna is usually nice.*
C. *There is a place called Buna-Buna.*

Although all of these conclusions might be suggested by the given fact, only the third is fully justified.

Example Ten

Let us take one more example — a task that is based upon *Figure 1.6*. A girl is looking in a mirror and apparently fixing her hair. What things are most wrong with this picture, or most unlikely?

Figure 1.6

The girl is holding a tennis racket in her hand, while apparently checking on the condition of her hair, which is an unlikely act, but not unthinkable. One of the drawer handles does not match the others, but it might be just a temporary replacement, or a substitute for a style that can no longer be found. The worst discrepancies are in the reflections in the mirror. For one thing, the style of the girl's hair shown in the mirror does not agree with her actual style. Other bad errors are in the reflections of her arm and hand. Her arm appears on the left, as she looks in the mirror, whereas it should appear on her right, as all ordinary mirrors would have it. Also, her hand should appear in front of her hair, as in all probability it is actually located.

The ten examples of test items or problems that have just been seen should give some idea of the variety and range of intellectual abilities. Each example features one particular ability. These ten are only a few out of a much larger number of abilities. As you probably have observed, there are some similarities between some pairs of tasks and therefore of their abilities. They can be classified in different ways, as you will see in later chapters.

HOW WE FIND COMPONENT ABILITIES

It is safe to say that no person is equally strong in all the intellectual abilities. Each person does better in some kinds of tasks than he does in others. It is from the unevenness of performance of individuals in different kinds of tests that psychologists have been able to discover the basic, or primary, abilities. They have administered to subjects, most often students, in great variety, hundreds of tests, each test emphasizing some particular kind of mental activity. If it is found that students in a large group (perhaps 200) are likely to have similar ranks in both of two different tests, it is concluded that the basic ability (or abilities) for doing these two tests is (are) the same. If students are high in the ability (or abilities), they are likely to make high scores in *both* tests. If they are low in the ability (or abilities), they are likely to make low scores in both. Moderate scores in the one test tend to go with moderate scores in the other. Tests of such a pair have a *positive correlation*.

Let us consider one of these tests paired with a third. In this pair it is found that the same student can have very different scores or ranks. The student may be high in the one, but anywhere from high to low in the other. These two tests have a zero (or near-zero) correlation. The conclusion is that these two tests depend upon very different abilities; they have essentially no ability in common.

Incidentally, rarely is there a genuine *negative* correlation between two tests of intellectual abilities. A negative correlation between two tests would mean that students who are high in one of them are more likely than not to be low in the other. There is sometimes a popular idea that negative correlations are common. For example, it may be thought that if a student is very good in gaining knowledge and in memorizing that knowledge, he is less likely to be good in reasoning or problem solving. If there is any relationship at all, it is probably positive. In the case of gaining and storing information in relation to problem solving, the reason is simple. You must have information to solve problems at all. But it *is* true that you could have a lot of knowledge and still be unable to make much use of it in solving problems. You will see why later in this book.

WHY YOU SHOULD KNOW ABOUT YOUR INTELLECTUAL RESOURCES

This book is about your intellectual abilities, which also means that it is about the nature of your mental activities. Why should you know about the nature of your mental activities? You should, for the simple general reason that "Knowledge is power." That is, knowing what you do intellectually gives you some control over your mental functioning. The proof of this proposition has been shown many times. One recent instance was with children in grades four to six. Insofar as they could understand the mental operations involved, they could use that knowledge in their learning and problem solving. After two months of this instruction their gains in mental abilities and in standard achievement tests were remarkable. Additional evidence will be cited in later chapters, particularly *Chapter 10.*

Some of the knowledge about intelligence can also be very useful in understanding people and in dealing with them. This last statement refers to a large set of abilities under the general heading of "social intelligence." Those abilities were brought to light only within recent years, and are still almost entirely missed by IQ tests.

Students are often told, by teachers or parents, that one of the important reasons that they go to school is to learn how to think. It is really quite interesting that those who have made such a statement usually have only a vague idea about what it actually means to think. To the average person, thinking is the same wherever we find it. What, then, is thinking? You will find answers to this question in this book. The term "answers" is used because there are many kinds of thinking, and suggestions for improving your thinking skills will follow.

WHAT IS INTELLIGENCE?

In the earliest use of the term by the Romans, intelligence meant information. To this day, in military affairs, it means information obtained by secret agents regarding the enemy. On occasion it has other applications in affairs of government. We shall have occasions to refer to the connection between intelligence and information, for it makes good psychological sense to connect the two, where information goes well beyond military affairs, of course.

The modern use of the word "intelligence" came from observations of the naturalists, the early biologists. They noticed that living creatures have two general ways of coping with their enivronments. Animals act either through what were called instincts, or through intelligence; one or the other. In the first case, they appear to inherit from their ancestors some behavior patterns for meeting very common situations in standardized, machine-like ways. It is as if their nervous systems had been programmed to operate in specified ways, and such programs are passed on in the genes of the species. Such acts are more clearly seen in the behavior of insects.

Although higher forms of animals, such as mammals (including man), also have some instinctive behavior patterns ready to function, for the most part, they have to learn *new* behavior patterns in order to cope with situations. They have to program themselves through experience. Psychologists commonly adopted this view of intelligence; that it is the ability to learn. When the individual has no ready-built response patterns to cope with a new kind of situation, he tries to develop a new way, a new program, for doing so. This is intelligent behavior.

This idea, rough as it is, seemed to be generally satisfying until psychologists developed what they called intelligence tests. The customary idea then seemed to be too broad and too vague, and they tried to get a better one. Lewis M. Terman, who developed the most popular intelligence scale, the Stanford-Binet, said that intelligence is the ability to do abstract thinking. But he did not succeed in defining either "abstract" or "thinking." And when we examine the tests that compose the Terman scale, we find that a large majority of them simply call for understanding or knowledge, as in vocabulary tests, while some others call for memory, as in memory-span tests (repeating short lists of digits, like telephone numbers, immediately after hearing them once). There is quite a jump from understanding and memorizing to "abstract thinking." We shall see later why this is so.

But other psychologists did not accept Terman's idea, nor did they agree with one another. One of them, E. G. Boring, essentially threw up his hands and said that intelligence is whatever intelligence tests test. This would have been a fair working definition, good for many purposes, except that different intelligence scales emphasized different abilities, and there would have been as many different intelligences as there were scales.

Boring's suggestion was definitely in the right direction, however, for it pointed to the need to find out what abilities are actually measured by different tests, all of which could be regarded as requiring intellectual activity. Fortunately, there was a known method by which one could find out mathematically what abilities are involved in doing the tests. It is known as *factor analysis*.

Factor analysis of intelligence into its component abilities has been vigorously pursued only within the past 35 years, and by only a handful of psychologists. But as of today, we have detailed, extensive information on the subject. There is still much work to be done on it. It turns out that there are far more different abilities than anyone had expected. But, fortunately, it has been possible to organize them in a single system known as the *Structure of Intellect*.

You will learn about this system or model, and will find that the principles involved will be very useful. You will learn what the different abilities mean in connection with your everyday learning, thinking, and problem solving. Knowing the nature of your abilities, you will be able to turn them on when you need them and you will learn how to exercise them in order to strengthen them.

SUMMARY

This book is about the numerous intellectual abilities that make up your intelligence. Ordinary IQ scales assess only a limited number of them, usually those most important for learning in school. Probably every person is uneven in his abilities. A person may be high in some, medium in others, and low in still others.

During the middle years of this century, some psychologists have used a method known as factor analysis for finding out what the component abilities of intelligence are. You should know something ⸱ about those abilities, for they are your intellectual resources and they provide suggestions as to how thinking skills can be developed and utilized. Furthermore, it will be seen that the abilities have been organized in a unitary system, whose features tell us a great deal about our mental functioning.

EXERCISES

1. Think of some person whom you know, or of some prominent person who appears to be strong in some abilities and weak in others. How has this been shown in his/her behavior?

2. Attempt to rate yourself on a ten-point scale with respect to how you think you stand on each of the ten abilities illustrated in this chapter, as you understand those abilities. Do the same for a friend whom you know well. Do the results tend to account for differences between you two in everyday performances?

3. Try the following two probems on your friends and watch for individual differences in the ways they do or do not solve them:

    a. A thermos bottle is standing in the sink, empty except for some ice cubes in the bottom. Your problem is to get the ice cubes out of the bottle. To make the problem more difficult, we shall specify that you may not turn the bottle over, and you have no tongs or other implements with which to fish the cubes out. Your hand is too large to enter the bottle. How can you get the ice cubes out of the bottle?

    b. A marble is dropped into a bottle, which is then

*corked. How can you remove the marble from the
bottle without touching the cork with anything?*

Such problems require some creative thinking, for the solutions are
rather novel. Probably anyone with a rudimentary education knows the
facts that are needed. He must bring those facts to bear on the problem,
using them in new ways. In problem *a*, you could fill the thermos bottle
with water and ice cubes would overflow at the top, or you could pick
them up. In problem *b*, you could break the bottle, assuming that it is
made of glass or some other breakable material.

Creative thinking requires some special intellectual abilities, which
have been discovered mostly within recent years. They are generally
missed by IQ tests. Those abilities will be treated in later chapters.

CHAPTER TWO

Major Kinds of Information: Contents

It was said in the preceding chapter that intelligence has an important connection with information. It should be asked then, "What, actually, *is* information and what does it have to do with intelligence?" We are concerned here, of course, with a much more general idea than that of military intelligence. Generally speaking, information is anything that we know. What *do* we know, when information is examined to discover its basic nature? In the next two chapters we will pursue the answers to that question.

FIGURAL AND SEMANTIC INFORMATION

You look out of the window and you see standing there a large, round green mass that you recognize as a tree. All over it are small, thin, plate-like objects fluttering about, from which you know that the wind is blowing. There was a time, in your infancy, when, looking out of the same window, you would have seen only a mass of uneven green and little more. You would not know what the object was. Information was limited to colors and shapes, but you were unable to identify or name colors and shapes.

At present you would have that same information also, but some other information is added concerning what *objects* are there and something about their natures. A botanist, viewing the same object, would have still more information. In these illustrations we have met two basic kinds of information. One kind is concrete or tangible; it is given to you immediately through your sense of sight. The other kind is entirely in your thoughts and is therefore sometimes called "abstract." It is extracted or abstracted secondarily from the concrete information. From now on in this book, concrete or perceived information will be referred to as "figural," and abstract, meaningful information as "semantic." Reasons for preferring these terms will be forthcoming.

Coding of Information

One very important fact about information is that it is constructed by our brains. It is easy to believe that the *idea* "tree" is a product of our brain activity. The idea does not exist in the object, although we assume, of course, that there is an object out there that calls forth the idea when the eye and the brain are exposed to it. The truth of the matter is that the figural information that we get from the object out there is also manufactured by our brains, coupled with activity of the eyes and the optic nerves. No tree and no green, as such, enter the eye and ride the nerves to the brain. What comes from the object is light energy of certain wave lengths and in certain spatial patterns. The eye focuses the incoming light waves upon the retina and the retina sends waves of electrochemical energy on to the brain, also patterned.

Everything is in code, like the signals coming from a television-transmitter station to your television set. The TV set decodes the message, as your brain decodes the incoming nervous impulses. There is a restructuring in a new "language," and some kind of facsimile of the original source object is produced. This is the visual-figural information.

The semantic information involved in your recognition of the object is in still a different language. There is a recoding from visual-figural to semantic information. The translation into semantic coding enables you to do much more with the object than if you were restricted to figural information alone.

It is now easier to explain the choice of the terms "figural" and "semantic." As pointed out, an item of information is organized or structured by the brain; it is a construct. It is easy to accept the idea that there is structure in things that you see. Visually perceived objects have not only shape and texture but also boundary lines and internal organization. The term "figural" thus naturally applies.

The term "semantic" comes from the field of semantics, which is concerned with meanings connected with words. This kind of information could have been called "verbal," since most meanings have words attached to them. But the trouble would be that many meanings exist without word labels. One common instance is in the young child who cannot yet talk and perhaps cannot understand speech but undoubtedly has semantic information, judging from his behavior. Even some speechless animals, like monkeys, appear to have semantic information. Undoubtedly on occasion you have ideas that you could not put into words. Thus, semantic information is in the form of meanings, verbalized or not.

What have figural and semantic information to do with intelligence? The answer is that we have found a great many abilities for dealing with figural information and a large number of parallel abilities for dealing with semantic information. Generally speaking, we may regard the figural abilities taken together as comprising a "concrete intelligence" and the semantic abilities as comprising an "abstract intelligence," although we shall not find these expressions particularly useful.

Thus far, this discussion has been limited to *visual*-figural information. There is good evidence also for a set of abilities for dealing with *auditory*-figural information. Man-made auditory-figural information is composed very largely of speech sounds and music. There may also be some figural abilities associated with other kinds of sensory input—kinesthetic, for example. The latter sense is concerned with feelings of bodily positions and movements. There is structured information from the sense of touch, indicated by the fact that we recognize objects from that source alone and more dramatically by the fact that the blind learn to read Braille.

Meaning

It was said that semantic information equals meaning, so let us take a closer look at meaning. Consider the printed word "tapir," for example; a word not often encountered. If you do not know what this word means, you lack the semantic information to go with the printed symbol that you recognize as a word but it might as well be in a foreign language.

If you go to the dictionary to look up the word, you will find something to the effect that the tapir is a large, nocturnal ungulate. If you look up the word "ungulate," you find that it is an animal with hooves. What the definition does is to put the tapir in the classes to which it essentially belongs. The largest class is that of "animals." Some animals have hooves and some do not. The tapir belongs in the subclass "ungulates." It has hooves, like a horse, a sheep, or a moose. Ungulates can be of different sizes. The tapir is in the sub-subclass of "large ungulates." A few of the large ungulates come out to feed at night, among them the tapir. The class "nocturnal" is the smallest subclass. Along with the other class placements it narrows things down to restrict the meaning closer to the particular object. The class memberships for the tapir are illustrated in the diagram in *Figure 2.1* by means of concentric circles, showing class within class.

Placement of an item of information within essential classes gives us *denotative* meaning. It includes the essentials for identifying the object. But a dictionary frequently adds other helpful information, contributing to richness of meaning. This addition is known as *connotative* meaning.

Figure 2.1

A diagram showing the nature of the meaning of the word "tapir." The overlapping circles show placement within classes and subclasses to provide *denotative* or defining information. Other classes outside the largest circle are not essential for defining purposes but add *connotative* context and richness of meaning.

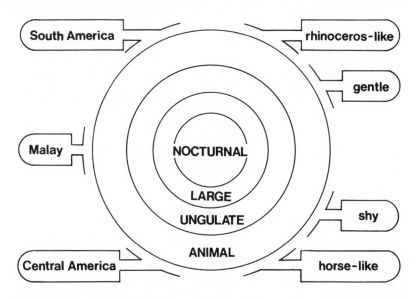

Regarding the tapir, the dictionary may also say that it is found mostly in Central and South America, with some in Malay. It is related to the horse and the rhinoceros. It is shy and gentle.

The added descriptions do give more class memberships for the tapir. It is in the class of things living in the countries mentioned; it is in the classes of horse-like and rhinoceros-like; and it is in the classes of shy and gentle things. In *Figure 2.1* these classes are shown as standing apart from the denotative categories.

All of these features are organized like a context about a core. If, in addition to all the contextual information already mentioned, you saw a picture of a tapir, its image (visual-figural information) would be added. If you were for some unusual reason ever startled by a tapir, the emotion of fear would be added to your meaning construct. We shall see later that feelings and emotions are also kinds of information. It should be added that when you think "tapir" not all the context comes to mind; perhaps only what you need at the moment.

The classes within classes picture of meaning is clearest in connection with objects. Other kinds of definitions are in terms of synonyms—words of similar meanings. They are in the same classes as the words defined. Still other definitions name attributes, but each' of them refers to a class. Thus, *meaning is a composite of associated attributes or of class memberships.*

In connection with this view of meaning, it is interesting that some 40 years ago Professor Robert P. Crawford at the University of Nebraska was concerned about teaching his students, primarily in journalism, how to think creatively. He called his favorite method of developing creative thinking "attribute listing." Attribute listing for an object, event, or idea means just what the expression clearly says: stating different attributes or properties that the thing in question possesses.

How can this activity contribute to creative thinking? In the operation of attribute listing, we are building up an increasingly richer meaning. The secret is that this makes the concept more useful to us. In creative thinking we are using information that we know in a variety of new ways. The effects should show up in creative writing and in other places as well—designing, inventing, planning, and problem solving.

In any of these creative activities, we are faced with the need for searching in our memory stores (our personal "vest-pocket" libraries). The denotative attributes organize our stored information in logical ways. Classes and subclasses are logical filing systems. "Is your mind a file or a pile?" is a question which was commonly seen in advertisements for memory courses. It is a very significant question. A well organized memory storage helps us to zero in on an idea of information that we want to retrieve and it also helps us to communicate accurately.

The connotative attributes, however, give color and even fascination to one's writing. We shall see in later connections that some of these attributes are so unusual and far-fetched that they not only contribute to figures of speech but they also lead to originality. A rich aura of connotations provides depth of meaning, and depth of meaning contributes to greater usefulness of semantic information.

In daily life the kinds of people who depend more strongly than others on semantic information are writers, speakers, teachers, planners, and scientists, to name some outstanding groups. Whether we are scientists or not, we map our world in terms of semantic items of information, and from this mapping we plan courses of action. Communication with others is mostly designed to arouse in them some duplication of our own semantic information. It can also add to stimulation of others emotionally as well as intellectually.

SYMBOLIC INFORMATION

So much has been said in these pages about communication that it is time that we took a closer look at the process itself. In doing so, we find a third kind of information known as "symbolic." Symbols ordinarily stand for something else; they are signs or tokens. Our most common symbols are composed of letters or numbers, as in words and telephone numbers. A letter or a number that is seen in print is first of all some visual-figural information. It has shape and size as well as orientation. But when a number, letter, or printed word is recognized as standing for something else, or when we manipulate numbers and letters as in mathematics, they become symbols.

For the person who has not learned to read, figural information is all he would get from a printed word. When the particular combination of letters becomes familiar to him and has an identity of its own, he has achieved a visual symbol. If he knows what the word means, he also has semantic information attached to it. The process of reading thus involves three kinds of information, and translations from figural to symbolic to semantic coding.

In his beginning to learn to read, the child is also concerned with *auditory*-symbolic (speech) information, which complicates things further. With so many different abilities involved, and with the fact that a serious defect in any link in the chain may cause difficulty, it is no wonder that there are so many children with reading problems. IQ tests tell us nothing about most of these abilities. It often takes careful testing and diagnosis to pinpoint the kind of difficulty. Knowing the several different abilities involved should help considerably in this step. Such abilities will be described in later chapters.

In addition to the common use of symbolic information in communication, there are certain people for whom symbolic abilities are of special importance. Mathematicians come first to mind. With some exceptions, as in geometry, mathematics is a special language composed of letters and numbers and other signs exclusively. Mathematical expressions and equations are manipulated according to "rules of grammar." Another group of people deal with coding problems, as in military affairs. They invent and decipher codes. Shorthand is a special symbolic code. Musical notation is another.

Translations into and out of symbolic codes are very common events. The teacher of mathematics instructs his students by putting mathematical ideas into semantic form and then into verbal-symbolic form, in order to communicate them. The textbook uses printed words for the same purpose. The student reads a problem in English and is told to translate it into symbolic form (an equation) in order to solve it mathematically. Skills in making such translations, like all skills, must be developed by practice. Incidentally, in this brief discussion of translations we can see the analogy to learning foreign languages.

BEHAVIORAL INFORMATION

How well do you understand people and how well do you understand yourself? How well can you influence or manage others to get them to do what you would like them to do? Such understandings and such management involve still another interesting kind of information called "behavioral." It is concerned with what people feel, think, and intend to do in their dealings with other people.

In a social gathering you are aware not only of the appearances of individuals and of what they are saying but also of what attitudes they have, what relations they have with others in the group, and the interplay of feelings. All of these things are items of behavioral information. It is a different kind, for we know that the abilities for dealing with it are different. This does not mean that you do not have the other kinds of information in the same situation, for you *are* aware also of other peoples' shapes, features, and dress, and you have ideas about their names, ages, and so on; in other words, you possess both symbolic and semantic information. Some of the figural information gets translated directly into behavioral information, as when the facial expression you see becomes translated into feelings. Smiles and frowns indicate pleasure and displeasure. From such expressive signs and from what individuals say, and how they say it, we have another mode of communication between persons. Some call it "body language." It is *nonverbal* communication that skips semantic and symbolic links that would otherwise be used. For some examples of body language, see *Figure 2.2.*

This distinct category of information entails a large number of abilities that come under the general heading of "social intelligence." Most probably you have observed that some of your friends are quite adept at understanding others and perhaps also in managing them. You may also have noticed that some people are good at understanding others but not so good at managing them, or vice versa, although the latter variation is not so likely. These are examples of levels of social intelligence which may, by the way, be fairly high without high academic intelligence or IQ. Even some mentally deficient persons (of low IQ) make surprisingly good social adjustments, which may be due to their higher status in behavioral abilities.

Behavioral abilities are obviously especially important for people who must deal effectively with others. Among occupational groups for

Figure 2.2
Some simple examples of expressive faces, which, even in this crude form, convey behavioral information to the viewer. Try naming the mental state of each person. Ask a friend to do the same. How well do you agree?

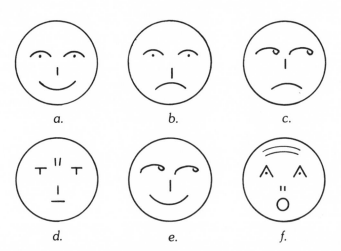

which this is true are teachers, salesmen, politicians, statesmen, supervisors, policemen, lawyers, judges, probation officers, and social workers. All parents would be more successful in bringing up their children if they had strong behavioral abilities. Gang leaders no doubt gain and hold their positions as leaders because of them. Incidentally, a psychologist who worked with juvenile delinquents came to the conclusion that there are at least two important types of delinquents. One of the groups tends to be rather low in social intelligence. Its members tend to misinterpret their social environments, consequently get into trouble or are easily led into it. They do not see that others are manipulating them. The other type tends to be high in social intelligence, so its members can, and do, manipulate their associates, their parents, and others in authority over them.

INFORMATION AND INTELLIGENCE

It is time to consider the connection between information and intelligence. Having seen some examples of different kinds of information it is easier to appreciate what information is. The most striking thing about information is that each item is different from every other item, at least different enough that we can distinguish one from the other. Where we can make no distinction there is no information. We take a cue here from the communication engineers, who deal with the transmission of information from a sender to a receiver. They have offered the definition that information is "that which is discriminated." That is also our basic definition here. The more discriminations you make, the more information you have.

But intelligence is more than a matter of having information. We may look upon our brains as being elaborate computers between our ears; more elaborate than any yet constructed by man, and definitely more compact. Their main purpose is the processing of information. Like electronic computers, brains have memory stores that preserve records of our experienced information. They receive information through input channels; they decode it and recode it. They store it and later retrieve it, generating new information as in problem solving. This new information may also be put into memory storage. Thus, we may say that *intelligence is a collection of abilities for processing information of different kinds in various ways.* The basic operations in processing will be treated in chapters to come.

An important question concerning informational content needs a little more consideration here. Why do all the kinds of content that were mentioned have some relation to intelligence? This question applies most to figural and behavioral information. You may recall the question whether the figural abilities cited in connection with pilot training in the preceding chapter are intellectual. There have also been mentioned a "concrete intelligence" and a "social intelligence." Although visual-figural abilities have had some representation in standard IQ tests, behavioral abilities have not. Briefly, the best excuse that can be given at this stage is that we find in these two areas abilities that are completely parallel with those in the semantic and symbolic areas.

Before leaving the subject of informational contents, it may be pointed out that the interests of high-school and college students tend to differ along the lines of the content categories. Some students are most interested in dealing with concrete things; things they can see or hear. Some students are more attracted to ideas as in the sciences or the humanities. We might say they are "semantic-prone." Others show attractions toward symbolic information, as in mathematics or languages. Still others are "turned on" by people, showing that they are "behavior-prone." Such knowledge may be of some use in vocational choices and vocational guidance.

SUMMARY

In this chapter we have seen that information comes in four major categories: *figural* (perceived through the senses), *symbolic* (signs or tokens), *semantic* (thoughts), and *behavioral* (mental states). These kinds of information are different codes or "languages" and there are translations from one to another. Communication with other persons is done mostly through the code of symbolic information but also to some extent through expressive behavior, a nonverbal code.

Information is defined as "that which we discriminate." It is structured. Information is connected with intelligence when that term is defined as a collection of abilities for processing different kinds of information in various ways. Parallel sets of abilities apply to the different content categories.

EXERCISES

If you should like to verify your understanding and your readiness to apply the kinds of informational content, the following problems should be of interest.

Problems:

1. In what kinds of content does each of the following groups of people most commonly deal in their occupational activities? One or two kinds are usually dominant. Give reasons.

   a. motion-picture director
   b. orator
   c. labor organizer
   d. poker player
   e. dentist

2. What kinds of content are most involved in the following activities?

   a. doing crossword puzzles
   b. solving mechanical puzzles
   c. playing chess or checkers
   d. diagnosing a friend's emotional problem
   e. solving arithmetical problems

Answers to problems:

1. Most common content for occupations:

   a. Motion-picture director—behavioral (interprets play's personal situations); visual-figural (plans arrangements of actors on stage)
   b. Orator—semantic (composes and remembers content of his oration); behavioral (tries to stir people and senses their reactions)
   c. Labor organizer—behavioral (is a leader of people); semantic (makes meaningful plans)

    d. Poker player—symbolic (keeps account of card values); behavioral (interprets reactions of his opponents)

    e. Dentist—visual-figural (perceives arrangements of teeth, tools, etc.; works looking in a mirror)

2. Most common content for activities:

    a. Cross-word puzzles—symbolic (spelling and fitting words within spaces); semantic (understands definitions given)

    b. Mechanical puzzles—visual-figural (seeing spatial arrangements of parts and imagining movements)

    c. Chess or checkers—visual-figural (seeing spatial arrangements; imagining next moves)

    d. Diagnosis—behavioral (grasping what kind of "hang-up" friend has)

    e. Arithmetical problems—semantic (understanding the problem); symbolic (doing numerical operations)

SUGGESTED READINGS

Readers who would like to pursue the topic of the nature of information further may find the following books of interest:

Ogden, C. K. & Richards, I. A. *The meaning of meaning.* NYC: Harcourt, Brace & World, 1930.

Cherry, C. *On human communication.* NYC: Wiley, 1957.

CHAPTER THREE

The Structure of Information: Products

The kinds of structures that information takes are called "products," to remind us that they are constructed by our brains. Where the different kinds of content are regarded as codes or languages, the products are something like parts of speech within a language. To continue the analogy, *particular* products are like words that compose a vocabulary. Each one is a particular item of information.

There are six kinds of products: *units, classes, relations, systems, transformations,* and *implications.* These same six kinds occur in *each* of the content categories.

UNITS OF INFORMATION

All items of information may be regarded as coming in chunks, of which units are the clearest examples. A unit is like an object or thing. It is a basic kind of product, for while it can stand alone, others are dependent upon it in one way or another.

Figural Units

In the visual-figural area, a unit could be just a patch of color, separated from its background by more or less distinct boundary lines; or it could be a large, elaborate object, such as the image of a house. But we can see parts of the house as units—roof, wall, door, window, or even a window pane. By analysis we produce smaller, simpler units. Keeping this illustration entirely within the visual-figural code, it is only such things as color patches, boundaries, shapes, and sizes that contribute to its classification as to content.

In the auditory-figural area the best examples of units are found in music and speech. Units could be single musical tones or musical chords. In speech the elementary sounds, called "phonemes," are among the simplest units. Larger units are spoken words. Among expressive vocalizations are chuckles, sighs, grunts, groans, and screams. In nature there are sounds of thunder, crackles, swishes, and squeaks.

Symbolic Units

Symbolic units parallel some of the figural ones just mentioned. Either a printed or handwritten syllable or word is in the symbolic category. The same is true of speech sounds when they are taken as labels referring to something else. For completeness it should be added that single letters or numbers can also become symbolic units, as when we speak of group A, or football player number 38, and so on. And then there are some conventional signs such as $, &, and ?. Like letters and numbers, each of these items has its figural aspect, as when it is taken as a line or set of lines especially by a person who has not yet been initiated to their symbolic references.

Semantic Units

The clearest examples of semantic units are familiar objects; not the way they look but the way in which they are known to us, with all their known features. There are also intangible ideas, such as love, justice, truth, readiness, and the like. Like tangible objects they are labeled with nouns. But some semantic units can be labeled with adjectives—smart, lazy, kind, or wholesome. Some can also be labeled with adverbs—rapidly, carefully, fully, or candidly.

Behavioral Units

Behavioral units include feelings and emotions, such as pleasure, tension, effort, anger, terror, and disgust. There are certain other states of mind, such as attention, reflection, doubt, or determination, and there are intentions—to caress, to strike, to ask, or to relax. All such units of information are communicated by what people say or do, especially in what we call expressive behavior.

CLASSES

It is not news to you that things can be grouped together in classes because they have one or more attributes in common. As a matter of fact, anything has identity because it has its own combination of properties, and every property it has puts it in a different class. We saw in the preceding chapter how putting an object in classes gives it meaning that is called semantic information. Classes provide the most common basis for organizing our information and we shall see that they play very important roles in memory and thinking.

Figural Classes

We can illustrate visual-figural classes by using capital letters. What are the common visual features in each of the following four-letter sets? Try to decide what the common properties are before reading further.

1.	O	S	C	U
2.	A	H	L	T
3.	Z	N	A	K
4.	P	D	B	R
5.	H	F	N	Z

Sometimes the members of a letter set here have more than one property in common. The common features are as follows: *(1)* only curved lines; *(2)* each has a horizontal straight line; *(3)* at least one acute angle, or each has one or more slanting lines; *(4)* each has a loop, or each contains both straight and curved lines; and *(5)* each contains parallel lines.

Spoken words can be classified according to similarity of sounds, to form auditory-figural classes. In the sample items that follow, you should speak the words or imagine how they sound. In each set of words three of them have similar sounds and can therefore belong to the same class. In each case which word does *not* belong to the class?

	a	*b*	*c*	*d*
1.	roam	dome	some	foam
2.	light	eight	flite	sight
3.	come	sum	dumb	dome
4.	dim	time	rhyme	climb

The right answers to problems 1 to 4 are c, b, d, a, respectively. It is clear that a poet must have some of this ability to classify sounds, unless he is permitted to take considerable "poetic license."

Symbolic Classes

Examples of symbolic classes may be seen in the following sets of printed words. It is common properties with respect to word composition or spelling that makes the class members symbolic rather than either figural or semantic.

1.	TOOTH	TASTE	TREE
2.	WHEN	ENTER	CENT
3.	MADAM	TREAT	RATHER

Examination of the class members in the sets will show that the following class ideas apply: *(1)* each word begins with *T;* *(2)* each word contains *EN;* *(3)* each word begins and ends with the same letter.

Semantic Classes

In daily life we are most commonly aware of classes of meaningful objects. Here are a few examples, some very easy to see, some not so easy:

1.	*CARROT*	*TURNIP*	*POTATO*
2.	*CUP*	*BOWL*	*PLATE*
3.	*DESK*	*SOFA*	*RADIO*
4.	*CAMERA*	*RADIO*	*TYPEWRITER*

The class ideas are: *(1)* vegetables, *(2)* dishes, *(3)* furniture, and *(4)* mechanical devices.

Behavioral Classes

Behavioral classes could be illustrated by using sets of facial expressions, use of hands, or body postures. The following examples are based upon verbal comments, each to indicate the state of mind of the speaker:

1. *Just what I wanted. Success at last. So glad to see you.*
2. *How horrible. You're a damn liar. He's revolting.*
3. *Get out of here. I'm leaving at once. Keep out of my sight.*

Behind the first set of remarks we see reactions of pleasure as providing the common element. The second set indicates some violent, unpleasant emotions in common. Attitudes behind the third set are of rejection, withdrawal, and avoidance, all of which involve putting distance between the speaker and someone else.

RELATIONS

Relations are kinds of connections between units. You can say what those connections are, if you recognize them and you know the words with which to communicate them. With two things connected, there are three items of information involved—two units and the relation between them. The three taken together will be called a "relationship" in what follows.

Figural Relations

In the visual-figural area there are said to be only about a dozen basic relations, but there may be more than that. The same relation can occur between different pairs of units; it is *transposable*. Some examples of visual-figural relations are shown in *Figure 3.1*. First try to see the relation in the top pair, then suggest what figure is needed to replace the question mark in order to complete the relationship in the bottom pair. The relation of *b* to *a* is to be the same in both rows.

Figure 3.1

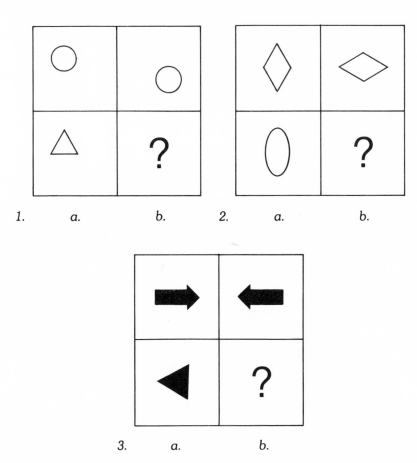

In the following key to the right answers, for each problem the kind of relation is stated, followed by a description of the unit that is needed to complete the second relationship:

1. *b is lower than a and to the right; a triangle at the lower right.*
2. *b is horizontal where a is vertical, or b is a turned 90 degrees; a horizontal ellipse.*
3. *b is a mirror image of a, or b is a flipped over to the right; a black triangle with one angle pointed to the right.*

Common relations found in auditory-figural information are musical intervals, such as octaves, fourths, or fifths. There are also major and minor keys. In speech as well as in music we encounter relations of "higher than" (with reference to pitch), "louder than," and "faster than." Incidentally, these relations illustrate how we can obtain *variables,* in these particular cases the variables of pitch, loudness, and tempo. Thus, quantitative relations such as "more than" give us ideas of continuous variables. Other simple examples are the visual variables of length, area, angle, and brightness.

Symbolic Relations

The following problems illustrate some of the many possible relations that exist between letters, words, and numbers. In mathematics the kinds of relations are almost endless. In each problem below the same relation is given two times between different units, in order to make more certain that the relation will be seen. The third relationship is only started. Try to see what *b* term is needed in each case:

	a	*b*	*a*	*b*	*a*	*b*
1.	grand	ran	merry	err	claps	?
2.	ton	not	am	ma	deer	?
3.	4	16	3	9	2	?
4.	2	5	5	11	4	?

The right answers, and reasons for them are:

1. *lap (The b word is the same as the three middle letters of the a word; a whole-part relation is involved.)*
2. *reed (b is a spelled backwards.)*
3. *4 (b is the square of a.)*
4. *9 (b is 2 times a plus 1.)*

Semantic Relations

As you should expect, semantic relations are between meaningful units. The following problems are similar in form to those for the symbolic relations just given. What words should go in the blanks to show that you understand the relation in each problem?

	_a_	_b_	_a_	_b_	_a_	_b_
1.	hard	soft	up	down	dry	_?_
2.	peach	fruit	pea	vegetable	beef	_?_
3.	fish	swim	bird	fly	man	_?_
4.	hand	arm	hub	wheel	page	_?_

The answers and their reasons are:

1. *wet (b is the opposite of a).*
2. *meat (b is the natural class to which a belongs.)*
3. *walk (b is the natural mode of locomotion of a.)*
4. *book (b is the whole of which a is a part.)*

Behavioral Relations

Can you see what relations exist between members of the three pairs of people in *Figure 3.2?* The stick figures were intended to show that *A* loves *B* and *B* loves *A* in return, a two-way relationship. *C* dominates *D*, giving him a lecture and a headache. *E* is trying to impress *F*, and is apparently doing so.

Figure 3.2

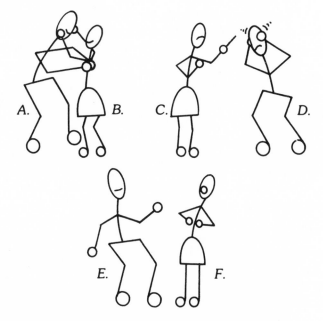

SYSTEMS

In terms of the numbers of units, also relations or classes, involved, systems are the most complex items of information. They are composed of more than two interconnected units. Whereas two units are sufficient to give us a relation, it takes more than two units and often more than one relation to form a system.

An order or sequence of units is a very common kind of system. In this case only one relation is sufficient—before-and-after. The alphabet is such a system, with many units but one relation. The number system has not only order but a wealth of interrelations, some of which are still being discovered. A mechanical or electric device, such as a television set, is a very complex system. To the extent that we grasp the inner connections of all these things we have informational systems.

Figural Systems

In visual-figural information, the most common system we have occurs every time we open our eyes and see the arrangements of things in space around us. Things come in order within that space. In three-dimensional space, the common relations are conceived as being right-left, up-down, and near-far or front-back. Our own body is usually conceived as being within the system and as providing the frame of reference. The physical scientist gets away from his own body as the frame of reference, for which he substitutes other frames, such as mathematical coordinates or astronomical landmarks. In his thoughts the mathematician conceives of four and even more dimensions, but this gets him over into the semantic area of information.

Some simple problems involving visual-figural systems are given in *Figure 3.3*. Each pair of cubes presents a problem. The problem is to decide whether or not the two cubes could be identical. They are identical only if letters that can be seen on their faces have the same arrangement in the two views. In problem 1, the two cubes could be the same. The R and the V bear the same relation in both cubes. In problem 2, the cubes cannot be the same, for T and D are not arranged in the same way. In problem 3, A and U are turned differently. In problem 4, the J and N are similarly related in both cubes.

Some very clear examples of auditory systems can be given from music. Melodies and rhythms are the most familiar examples. More complex systems are found in musical arrangements, which give melodies additional complexity, especially when played by orchestras.

Quite likely, we should find that there are kinesthetic systems, to mention another sensory area. Such systems would be seen in

Figure 3.3

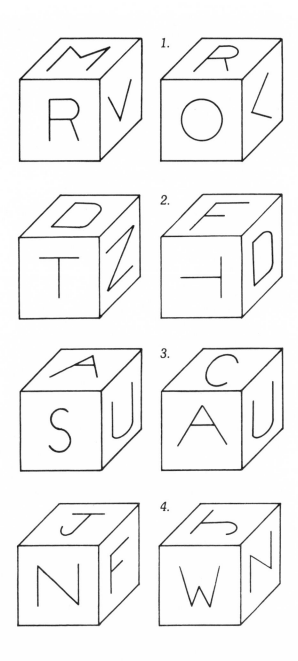

connection with artistic dancing. To the performing dancer, felt patterns of movement parallel the music to which he or she dances. Skilled athletes also learn patterns of movement that when performed "feel right," while other patterns do not. The patterns of kinesthetic sensation that are felt are figural systems. Communicating these patterns, from coach to student, presents some special problems. Only considerable practice can produce the desired patterns or systems of Olympic quality, or those of a concert pianist.

Symbolic systems

It is much easier to display symbolic systems. They can be readily constructed of letters or numbers, which can be organized in numerous ways. Consider the following letter series:

1. *A   D   G   J   M   P   ?*
2. *T   S   R   Q   P   O   ?*
3. *A   Z   B   Y   C   X   ?*

Show that you have grasped each system by adding one or two letters in each case. The letters needed, with reasons, are:

1. *S   V   (Starting with A, every letter skips two in alphabetical order.)*
2. *N   M   (Letters are in reversed alphabetical order, starting with T.)*
3. *D   W   (The odd-numbered letters in the series are in the forward alphabetical order and even-numbered letters in backward alphabetical order.)*

Now look at some number series. Decide what the principle is in each given series and show that you have seen it by supplying the next two numbers:

a.	*2*	*5*	*8*	*11*	*14*	*?*
b.	*3*	*6*	*12*	*24*	*48*	*?*
c.	*5*	*3*	*9*	*7*	*21*	*?*

The answers to these problems, with principles, are:

a.   17   20   (Add 3.)
b.   96   192   (Multiply by 2.)
c.   19   57   (Alternately subtract 2 and multiply by 3.)

As a general comment about systems it should be pointed out that although they are composed of units and relations, and sometimes classes, it takes special abilities to deal with them. Abilities for dealing with units or relations or classes alone are not sufficient for dealing with systems. Systems are something more than the elements that compose them. The same system can exist in different sets of units. For example, a melody can be played in different octaves. It is still the same melody. The letter and number series given above could begin with other letters or numbers; the principle would be the same. Like a relation, a system is transposable; it is a ghostly something that becomes embodied with different combinations of elements. It is like the grin without the cat that Alice saw in Wonderland.

Semantic Systems

Semantic systems are organized thoughts. A common example is a sequence of events that is observed. In the course of a half-day, a student eats breakfast, bicycles to school, attends certain classes according to schedule, visits the school principal, and goes to the library to study. If someone later asks him how he spent the day, he could relate the events in the right order. Thus, an individual's orientation with respect to events in time is a matter of semantic systems, just as orientation with respect to space is a matter of visual-figural systems, and an orientation to a mathematical expression or equation is a matter of symbolic systems.

Another common example of semantic systems is a problem that we comprehend, like an ordinary arithmetical problem, verbally stated. Consider a very simple case:

If you can buy two colas for 15 cents, how much would eight colas cost?

This problem system involves two quantities of colas (2 and 8) and two quantities of money. One of the latter is given and the other is to be found by the problem solver. He can solve the problem if (1) he grasps the combination of related pairs so that he knows what numerical operations must be performed, and (2) he performs the operations correctly. He may conceive of the problem in this somewhat standard manner: *2 is to 15 as 8 is to what?* Or, his conception might be verbalized: *8 colas will cost 4 times as much as 2 colas.* In these conceptions of the problem the structure is still semantic. However, when the solver thinks *"8 is 4 times 2"* and *"15 times 4 is 60,"* he is dealing with symbolic information. There is no law that says that a problem-solving event is confined to one kind of informational content.

In one kind of test problem we can avoid the involvement both in numerical operations and in symbolic information. Take the following problem, for example:

> A rectangular tank is being built to hold water. It is to
> be 5 feet wide and 9 feet long. How many cubic feet of
> water will it hold?

The problem is not to give a numerical answer but to say what other fact is needed to solve the problem. The answer should be, *"the height of the tank."* Giving this answer would show that the problem is understood; that the system is grasped.

Such problems can, of course, be much more complex. In the problem just given, we could ask for the amount of water in gallons, for example. With this much complication we need to know a second unstated fact — the number of gallons to a cubic foot. As a general principle, wherever some degree of complexity is involved, there is need for seeing the structure as a system. Some individuals can master highly complex systems while others are limited to the comprehension of the simplest.

Behavioral Systems

As in other content areas, it takes more than two components to make a system. Where we can use two persons interacting to illustrate a relation, as shown earlier, it takes more than two to make a system. In sets of three people, one can often find examples of behavioral triangles. For example, A and B are both in love with C but with different expectations and intentions involved. C is not "turned on" by A, but trusts him. She is intrigued by B but is somewhat fearful of him.

The possibilities of different patterns of interpersonal relations are perhaps not endless but very great in number. A four-person system has additional possibilities and a multipersonal political organization could present most complicated patterns of feelings, attitudes, and intentions. The same is true of a collection of nations, friendly or unfriendly, strong or weak, and belligerent or peaceful.

A common cartoon strip provides another example of a behavioral system. Each panel of the strip may present a social situation with some degree of complexity, thus providing a system. The whole sequence usually tells a short story, which presents a larger system. Any story plot that deals with personal feelings and attitudes is a behavioral system, best seen in what is called a psychological novel. The nonbehavioral aspects of a story provide a semantic system. As the storyteller paints verbal pictures of scenes and stage settings for the reader to imagine, visual-figural systems are developed. Thus, the reader has systems in three different codes.

TRANSFORMATIONS

A transformation is any kind of change in information. We may observe the change as it happens, as in a drama or a motion picture, or we may know an item before and after a change, which gives us the knowledge that a change has occurred. The change itself is an item of information. Transformations may occur in any content area, also in other kinds of products.

Figural Transformations

In *Figure 3.4* two kinds of change apply to the four pairs of figures. In some pairs only a rotation of the object occurs, as if you were merely sliding a bit of cardboard around on the page, in going from view *a* to view *b*. In other pairs the object is turned over and its other side is showing in view *b*. In which pairs has only a rotation occurred? This is true of pairs 1 and 3. In pairs 2 and 4 there must be a turning over. You have to imagine the figure in motion, and this particular motion is the transformation.

Figure 3.4

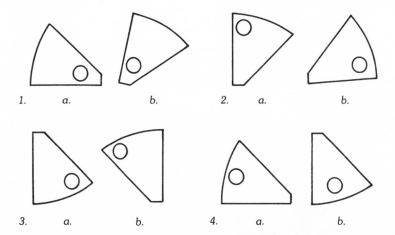

1.   *a.*   *b.*   2.   *a.*   *b.*

3.   *a.*   *b.*   4.   *a.*   *b.*

The ability to do this task, and similar ones, has been called "visualization." As you can well believe, visualization is very important for pilots of small aircraft and for others who manipulate mechanical equipment, also for visual artists, architects, and mechanical draftsmen, all of whom are concerned with imagining movements of objects in space or imagining rearrangements.

Auditory transformations can be found in music. Transposing a melody from one octave to another or from one key to another provide two examples. Variations on a theme provide another. A musical performer who has a unique style produces his own deviations from the way in which the music was written. In speech there are changes in pitch, in accents, in timing, and in other ways, as by an actor who goes from his natural way of speaking to a dialect to suit his character.

Symbolic Transformations

Did you ever try to read words spelled backwards? In the following sentences the words are not only spelled backwards but the order of the words in sentences is also reversed. You are to show that you read the sentences correctly by doing the simple things that they tell you to do.

> *elcric a ward*
> *sthgie eerht etirw*
> *owt sulp owt dda*
> *nezod a ni selppa ynam woh*

All capitals and punctuation marks were intentionally omitted to avoid giving special cues. If you have made the proper transformations, you should do the following things: *Draw a circle. Write three eights. Add two plus two.* Answer the question *"How many apples in a dozen?"*

You may have heard of spoonerisms. In this phenomenon the speaker interchanges letters or syllables. A person is most likely to be guilty of this error in saying tongue twisters. If you can make the proper transformations, you will undo the transformations made by the speaker of these spoonerisms:

> *rining doom*
> *mightnare*
> *redding wing*
> *wripetyter*

If necessary, say the written words to yourself several times, and the meaning that the speaker intended will come. Since the sounds of the words are important in this kind of solution, some auditory-symbolic transformation is also going on. In case you have not yet made all the transformations, here they are:

> *rining doom — dining room*
> *mightnare — nightmare*
> *redding wing — wedding ring*
> *wripetyter — typewriter*

Transformations are found everywhere in mathematics. Transposing equations is a common example, as well as simplifying, factoring, and other kinds of changes in expressions and equations.

Semantic Transformations

The most common semantic transformations are in the form of shifts or substitutions of meanings. Many words in a language have several different meanings. If you see or hear the word "scale," you may first think of a device for weighing things, if there is no context or situation that would help to tie down the meaning. If you were asked to suggest other meanings, you might think of fish scales, musical scales, of scaling a wall, and so on. Likewise, the word "tip" might mean a pointed end of something, but on further thought it might mean to tip over, a tip for the waiter, or a tip on a horse race. These are all cases of substitution.

Such changes are the basis for puns. Here are a few examples:

- *The bird-loving bartender was arrested and charged with contributing to the delinquency of a mynah.*
- *College bred means a four-year loaf made from the old man's dough.*
- *A sign in a Texas restaurant reads "Remember the a la mode."*
- *A fad is in one era and out another.*

For those who appreciate puns it can be seen that semantic transformations provide one important source of wit and humor. The moment of transformation touches off laughter, or at least a chuckle to one's self. Transformations in other kinds of information may not produce humor but they often provide sudden delight as well as surprise. The event is sometimes called an "aha" moment or experience by some; others call it an "eureka experience."

For one explanation of the humor in puns we may turn to Sigmund Freud's theory of laughter. He suggested that we become irked at having to conform to conventional rules, such as those that govern language usage, and when we can "kick over the traces," so to speak, we feel a sudden glory, a very common trigger for laughter. This explanation seems to be relevant to this type of humor. There are other theories and other occasions for laughter.

How can we explain the person who claims to see nothing funny in puns or who declares that puns are the lowest form of wit? There are several possible answers. It may be that he is low in the ability to see semantic transformations. If he fails to see the transformation, there is nothing funny. He has lost the chance for "sudden glory." On the other hand, he may be so high in the ability that only very subtle puns challenge him and therefore amuse him. If the Freudian theory does apply, another reason may be that the person suffers no discomfort from language restraints, hence he experiences no relief from puns.

Another common example of semantic transformations is connected with the use of objects. The recognized use of an object is semantic information. Children often define objects in terms of their customary uses — pillows are to sleep on, hammers are to pound with, paper is to write on, and so forth. Transformations occur when objects are adapted to some new use, as when a screwdriver is used as a bandleader's baton, a book is used to hold up a window, or a pencil is used to punch holes. Such transformations often come in handy in practical situations.

Leading scientists have told us that they value transformation abilities very highly. They want to be ready to revise their ideas when new facts become available or when an old theory fails to work. They must be perpetually open to new ideas. As for all of us, doggedly holding to our pet ideas may render us blind to better ideas.

Behavioral Transformations

How often have you become aware of the fact that you have badly misinterpreted the mental state or the intention of another person? Your change in impression is a transformation in behavioral information. In no other area are we so likely to be in error. The reason is that our cues for this kind of information are so incomplete and undependable. Emotional expressions are not always faithful indicators and we misread them. Thus, needs for transforming our impressions of behavioral events are unusual.

The behavioral interpretation of what a person says is often open to different interpretations, depending upon his tone of voice and his inflections. Take the word "please," for example. It would be uttered with different expression depending upon the circumstances and the relation of the speaker to the listener. In saying "please" to his secretary, a boss is likely to do it in a certain fashion. In which of the following situations would the behavioral import of the same word be quite different?

1. *a girl to her teacher*
2. *a beggar to a stranger*
3. *a woman to a waiter*
4. *father to son*

In 3 and 4 there is likely to be little or no transformation because the speaker is in a similar position of authority over the listener. In 1 and 2, however, the roles are almost reversed, so the expression would be different — a transformed item of behavioral information.

IMPLICATIONS

The best single word equivalent for implication, as a psychological item of information, is "expectation." When object or event A leads to the expectation of B, A implies B. As an item of information, the implication is the fact that in some sense B belongs to A. Lightning leads us to expect thunder; sunset leads us to expect darkness; and a traffic violation, seen by a traffic officer, leads us to expect a citation.

Figural Implications

In *Figure 3.5* are some open or incomplete figures. What does each figure suggest beyond itself? What would you add to each one?

Figure 3.5

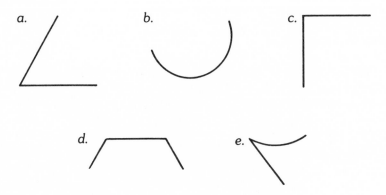

Whatever you add is implied by the information that is given. Here we see that an implication is an extension beyond what is given; an extrapolation. The term "suggests" is also naturally used here as an alternative for "implies."

It is fairly obvious that by adding one or more lines similar to those given in figures *a* through *d* we could complete some very familiar figures: triangle, circle, square, and hexagon, respectively. A complete, familiar object for figure *e* is not so obvious, but by adding a curve on top and a straight line at the right we could make a cone.

All such extensions complete the objects. There are other kinds of additions that could be made, some of them less obvious extensions. One kind of solution would be just to add one straight line connecting the loose ends of each figure, whether it made an object or not. On the other hand, we could add something more elaborate, using more than one or two lines. What is added, however, is most likely to take into account what is given. It would still be an implication in each case.

Symbolic Implications

Suppose the given information is the three-letter word ADA? What could be reasonably added to it? One might be impelled to extend the word, perhaps to make a longer one, such as ADAPT. Or, noting the symmetry of the given word, one might produce MADAM or the word RADAR, two other reasonable extensions.

If the given information is the series of numbers 8, 4, 2, what relevant additions could be made? Noting the principle in the series, we might merely extend it to read 16, 8, 4, 2, 1. Another quite different kind of solution would read $8 \div 4 = 2$. Mathematics is full of many and varied kinds of implications. Indeed, all the basic numerical operations are instances of implications. When a child learns his addition and multiplication tables he is acquiring sets of implications. For example, substituting the word "implies" for the equality sign, $3 + 9 = 12$ becomes $3 + 9$ implies 12; and $5 \times 6 = 30$ becomes 5×6 implies 30. Throughout mathematics, the "=" sign can be read "implies," or more accurately stated, "implies exactly."

Semantic Implications

One of the most common instances of implications in the semantic area is in the form of predictions. Present events forecast future events. The following problems call for some predictions. What would happen if:

1. *Beginning next year 20 percent more girls were born than boys?*
2. *A pill is found that cures all cancers?*
3. *Nothing any longer tastes sweet to human beings?*

Such problems are much more open than those in mathematics, in that for each one a number of different implications are not only possible but also reasonable. For problem 1, we could say that, in time, men would be outvoted; more women would be elected to office; the competition for husbands would be increased; and it might become legal for a man to have more than one wife.

For problem 2, we could say that there would be no more surgery for cancer; more people would die from other causes; and the proportion of elderly people would increase. The loss of a sweet taste in problem 3 would mean no more cultivation of sugar cane or sugar beets; less sugar in the diets; no more candy making and selling; and less tooth decay.

Behavioral Implications

Predictions of behavior would also be implications. What would person B be most likely to do or how would he feel if person A (1) winks at B; (2) points a finger at B, or (3) shakes his head vigorously at B? The outcome in each case would naturally depend upon other circumstances, such as the kind of person A is and the kind of person B is, and the kind of situation in which the stated action occurred. Allowing yourself all the possible circumstances, you could probably give quite a long list of relevant feelings and actions on the part of B in each case. All reasonable answers would be behavioral implications.

More on the Product of Implication

After seeing examples of implications in the different content areas, let us take a further look at the kind of mental structure an implication is. We started out with the idea that an implication is an expectation of one thing from another. In some illustrations, an implication was said to be an extension or extrapolation from what is given. The extension is in some way consistent with what is already given.

In other places it was said that there is an implication when one thing suggests another. Sometimes one thing suggests another because the two things are related, as in the instance of "shoe" suggesting "foot" or "day" suggesting "night." Not all implications depend upon relations, but those that do are more secure and the belongingness is more relevant.

Predictions were put in the category of implications. They are forms of extensions or extrapolations, as when we say that tomorrow's weather is likely to be like today's weather.

We may add here another kind of implication commonly known as a "conclusion" or a "deduction." If we are told that Tom is taller than David and Dick is shorter than David, we can certainly conclude that Tom is taller than Dick. If it is true that no native of Sabu Island smokes tobacco, then we know that Jigu, who is a native of that island, does not smoke tobacco. In each of these two examples, only one conclusion from the given information is logically permissible.

Implications of still another kind come under the heading of "elaboration." Elaborations are additions of detailed information. For example, an artist adds one brush stroke after another to his painting, even when to the casual observer the painting seems finished. Another example is the storyteller, who designs his plot in broad outline first and embellishes it with one detail after another. A planner organizes a skeleton of his plan, after which finer and finer details are added. All such additions are likely to be implications, suggested by, and consistent with, what has already been done.

USES OF PRODUCTS

How does it help us to know about the kinds of products of information? The values of this knowledge will become clearer in subsequent chapters, but something can be said here. Knowing the products of information and recognizing what kinds of products that we are dealing with can help in learning, remembering, and problem solving.

In learning something, our goal is clearer if we know more clearly what kind of product it is that we must acquire. Is it a unit, a relation, or a system? What kind of a system? What relations are involved? Or is it, perhaps, a transformation or an implication? What are the attributes of the thing that we are learning? In other words, what are its class memberships?

A good memory depends upon how information is put into memory storage. Things are better remembered and more easily recalled for future use if they are well organized. Things are organized by making use of various products of information. They may be related to other things; they may be put into classes or arranged in systems; or they may be associated, which means that implications are formed. It has been found that revising one's ideas (making transformations) helps to remember them. Information retrieval from storage is dependent on good cues that imply the information sought. Classes, relations, and implications are the most common sources of cues for retrieval.

In solving problems we depend very much upon information that is retrieved from our memory stores. We come to an understanding of the nature of the problem by making use of information in storage. In achieving understanding, we may need to generate several different hypotheses, which are implied by the given information. Our understanding of the problem leads us to see that the solution calls for a certain kind of product — a unit, relation, or system, for example. Perhaps none of the solutions we think of exactly solves the problem, but one item would do so if it were altered in some way — a transformation. Thus, all kinds of products can play their roles in problem solving, as will be explained much more fully in *Chapter 10*.

A PSYCHOLOGICAL MATRIX OF HUMAN KNOWLEDGE

The fact that all six kinds of products — unit, class, implication, relation, system, transformation — apply in all the categories of contents results in a cross classification. This system can be represented visually by the martix, or table of columns and rows, in *Table 3.1*. The content areas are represented by columns and the product categories by rows. Five columns times six rows yields 30 distinct kinds of information. With some possible exceptions we may say that this matrix of information includes every kind of knowledge that human beings possess.[1]

Table 3.1

A matrix of kinds of information.

CONTENTS

(V) Visual	(A) Auditory	(S) Symbolic	(M) Semantic	(B) Behavioral	PRODUCTS
VU	AU	SU	MU	BU	(U) Units
VC	AC	SC	MC	BC	(C) Classes
VR	AR	SR	MR	BR	(R) Relations
VS	AS	SS	MS	BS	(S) Systems
VT	AT	ST	MT	BT	(T) Transformations
VI	AI	SI	MI	BI	(I) Implications

In the table, each kind of content and each kind of product is symbolized by its initial letter with one exception. Semantic is symbolized by *(M)*, to avoid duplication and confusion with the *(S)* for the symbolic category. Within each cell in the table a combination of two letter symbols is given, with the symbol for content first. Additional advantage to this kind of labeling will be seen in the chapters that follow.

It should be noted that this matrix is a *psychological* model. There are other ways of classifying knowledge, as in a library. The system acquires added significance from the fact that associated with each cell there appear to be five similar abilities for dealing with information. This

---

[1]Earlier it was mentioned that there might be need for one or two additional figural columns. For example, from a few illustrations in this chapter there may be need for a column for auditory-symbolic information.

comes from the fact that there are five kinds of *operations* that we perform with information. In fact, all five different abilities have already been demonstrated by research within 16 of the 30 cells of the matrix, as well as two or more in each of several other cells.

SUMMARY

All human information is structured in the form of six kinds of psychological products. Our brains do the structuring in these six general forms. The basic kind of product is a *unit;* basic because other kinds of products partially depend upon it.

Units can be classified, giving rise to classes, or *class* ideas, a second kind of product. Units become tied in pairs, with some kind of connection between members of a pair. The most general kind of connection is an *implication,* another kind of product. There is an implication when one item of information leads to another, or suggests another. Sometimes the connection within the pair is more definite so that we have a known *relation.*

The most complex kind of product is a *system,* a combination of units or of other products interrelated in certain ways. A unique kind of product is a change of some kind, a *transformation.* This is a process or event, in which an item of information goes from one formation into another. Transformations contribute flexibility in information and information processing.

With six kinds of products in each of five kinds of content, we have a matrix of 30 different kinds of information. These 30 kinds cover almost everything that we know or can know.

Knowledge of the kinds of products can be useful because of their roles in learning, remembering, and problem solving.

EXERCISES

In *Chapter 1* some examples of test items were given to illustrate tasks featuring each of several different intellectual abilities. Most of those items are used here as problems by which you could test yourself regarding your readiness to see what products of information are involved. For each problem decide on the kind of product and also the kind of content.

Problems:

1. Similar expressions *(Figure 1.1)*
2. Identical blocks *(Figure 1.2)*

3. Monograms *(Figure 1.3)*
4. Associated names and numbers
5. Two faces *(Figure 1.4)*
6. Hidden letters *(Figure 1.5)*
7. Drawing conclusions
8. Errors in picture *(Figure 1.6)*

Answers to Problems:

The answers provided here are in terms of the symbols shown in *Table 3.1,* each followed by an explanatory note.

1. *BU (Identify the mental state.)*
2. *VT (Imaging the block turned around.)*
3. *VS (Letter arrangements are systems.)*
4. *SI (Connections between names and numbers.)*
5. *BR (Two persons with related feelings and attitudes.)*
6. *VT (Make parts of figure over into letters.)*
7. *MI (Conclusions are implications.)*
8. *MR (Related pairs of real objects.); also*
   MS (Arrangements of real objects.)

CHAPTER FOUR

What Do You Know?
Cognition

You have seen that there are at least 30 basic kinds of information with which we deal. Now the question is, what do we do with that information? How do we get it? How do we store it? How do we use it? And how can we tell how good it is? In this chapter, and in each of the four that follow, one of the five kinds of intellectual operations will be described and explained.

Cognition (the topic of this chapter) is the first and basic kind of operation. Once perceived, newly structured items of information may be stored in our brains by the next operation called *memory*. Stored items of information may be retrieved for future use as in problem solving. In retrieval are two different kinds of operations, because it matters whether the search of your memory store is a broad one or a narrow, focused one. If a broad one, in which you call up alternate items (in fact, you may be searching for a variety of alternatives), the operation is *divergent production*. On the other hand, if the search is focused in order to find a particular item, the operation is *convergent production*. We are perpetually checking on information that we know or that we have produced from our memory stores in order to determine its accuracy or its suitability, in an operation known as *evaluation*, the fifth intellectual operation to be discussed.

In the earlier chapters it was stated that the brain takes input from the sense organs and works it into the items of information, or products, that we know and remember. Discovering, knowing, and understanding are all instances of the operation of cognition. Because there are at least 30 kinds of information, as shown in the preceding chapter, there is a like number of cognition abilities, most of which have already been accounted for by research, and we know what kinds of tasks or tests require each of these abilities.

In what follows, we shall take up the abilities that are concerned with each kind of product of information in turn. For each ability we shall look at one or more kinds of test items that feature that ability. It is necessary to have these tangible examples in order to ensure good cognition of the operation of cognition.

Actually, throughout the previous chapter, you were encountering different cognition abilities when you were acquainting yourself with products of various kinds. Here, you will see many more examples of tasks involving the cognition of different kinds of products, but the emphasis will be on the operation. There are also special features of cognition that will be indicated.

COGNITION OF UNITS

Visual Units (CVU)[1]

How readily can you see and recognize familiar objects? With good daylight and with 20/20 vision, none of us has much difficulty. But under unfavorable conditions, as in dim lighting or with incomplete views, we have trouble at some time or other. The items in *Figure 4.1* are incomplete objects, not easy to recognize at first glance, although they are familiar objects. The first one is a sailboat and the second is an umbrella, neither one being very difficult to detect. But the third one is a different matter. It might be a dog or a cat, if you ignore the little line near the top of the frame which could hardly be a tail. The object intended is a toy wagon, such as children play with. The great amount of filling in one has to do in recognizing these incomplete figures demonstrates how much the brain has to do in perceiving objects. With more complete presentations we are not aware of this fact.

Symbolic Units (CSU)

How well can you identify familiar words under difficult viewing conditions? One task that illustrates this ability is known as the *Omelet Test*, in which the letters of words have been reordered, as in anagrams. What are the following words?

$$
\begin{array}{cccccc}
R & G & L & I & & \\
C & D & L & O & & \\
H & E & R & F & S & \\
H & C & W & I & H & \\
O & C & I & L & C & A \\
B & A & I & B & T & R \\
\end{array}
$$

---

[1]Each ability in the *Structure-of-Intellect* model (see *Figure 9.1*, p. 151) has a three-letter symbol, with kind of operation first, kind of content second, and kind of product third.

Figure 4.1

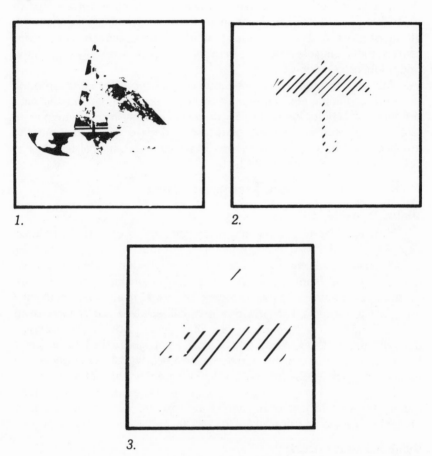

1.   2.

3.

In case you have not recognized all the words, they are: *girl, cold, fresh, which, calico,* and *rabbit.* Perhaps you had the most trouble with *"calico,"* because it is commonly the least familiar, which means that the brain has a less clear pattern in storage to provide help. In this we see the importance of stored information for ease of cognition.

Words can also be made difficult to cognize in another way, by removing their vowels, as in a test known as *Disemvoweled Words.* Here are a few "disemvoweled" words:

$$m - s - c$$
$$f - t\, h - r$$

$$c - l - n d - r$$
$$s p - c - c r - f t$$
$$c - n s t - t - t - - n$$

Printed in full the words are: *music, father, calendar, spacecraft,* and *constitution.*

It is easy to see why this ability should be more important for learning to read than is *CVU,* although the latter is basic to it. It is possible for a child to have little difficulty because he is adequate in ability *CVU* and yet fail because of low status in *CSU.* One time a boy of 11 was brought to a psychological clinic because he had never learned to read. One of the first tests given to him was for visual acuity. He looked at the chart on the wall and said, "I can't tell you what the letters are but I can draw them for you," and he did. He just did not know the letters as symbols.

Semantic Units (CMU)

How many word meanings do you know? In other words, how large is your reading vocabulary? Vocabulary tests are the best means for measuring ability *CMU.* Some vocabulary tests present words to be defined, as in the *Stanford-Binet Scale.* But the most common form presents each word and along with it a few alternative words, one of which means nearly the same as the given word. The following items contain some less common words:

1. *Amiable means — A. ethical   B. friendly*
   C. cooperative   D. helpful
2. *Arduous means — A. dangerous   B. different*
   C. tedious   D. untruthful
3. *Radiant means — A. shining   B. warm   C. degree*
   D. circular
4. *Cacophonous means — A. musical   B. exciting*
   C. entertaining   D. discordant
5. *Agglomeration means — A. crowd   B. infection*
   C. collection   D. mob

For items *1* through *5* the correct answers are: *B, C, A, D,* and *C.*

Vocabulary is important because knowing the meanings of words means the knowing of concepts. Concepts are important tools in thinking and in communication. It is no wonder that ability *CMU* dominates verbal IQ tests and scales. School learning contributes very much to *CMU* and, in turn, *CMU* contributes to further learning, for learning the new depends very much on what has been previously learned and stored. The relation of *CMU,* and hence the IQ, to school learning is shown by the fact that tests of knowledge of things learned in school are also measures of *CMU.* For example, general-information tests like the following can help to indicate the status of a person in *CMU:*

    1. What is the capital city of the Philippines?
      A. Hong Kong B. Tokyo C. Manila D. Jakarta
    2. From what element is nuclear energy derived?
      A. oxygen B. uranium C. aluminum D. fluorine

The answers, of course, are *C* and *B,* respectively.

But an education that stopped with the teaching of concepts, or merely semantic units, would be a very incomplete education. There are other kinds of products to be learned, which involve skills for using those units. Those skills involve operations other than cognition, also.

Behavioral Units (CBU)

How well can you know the state of mind of another person just from what you can see of his "body language," his posture, his facial expression, or how he holds his arms and hands? The items in *Figure 4.2* illustrate how we test for this ability. Given the expressive behavior in the drawing at the left, which of the four alternative expressions comes nearest to indicating the same state of mind?

In the *first item* the man at the left shows a positive stance, rigid and firm. The right answer is the upraised hand and pointing finger in alternative *3.* It is as if the person were making a point in a speech or argument. The upraised, clenched fist in *item two* suggests anger. The girl in answer number *4,* who is tapping her foot, suggests at least annoyance and is therefore the right answer. The man in *item three* seems to be making a jubilant, victory sign. The most likely answer to go with it is number *2,* the happy, laughing face.

Like other abilities, those in the behavioral area, including *CBU,* depend upon learning from experience for their development. If a child lacks opportunities for interacting with others, or is prevented from having normal personal contacts, his development in this area is likely to be retarded. It is not known whether interpersonal experiences at later ages can make up for such opportunities missed in childhood.

COGNITION OF CLASSES

The importance of classes was emphasized in *Chapter 3.* They are, indeed, a very important basis for the organization of all the information

Figure 4.2

Items from a test called *Expressions.*

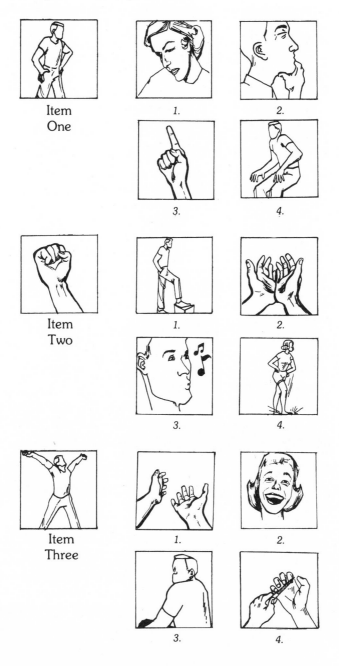

that we know. They are needed in the identification of units, and other kinds of products. Our brains are stocked with numerous class ideas and we cognize new information by assigning it to the proper class or classes.

Visual Classes (CVC)

Look at *Figure 4.3,* where five figural classes are represented with three members each, which we could describe in the following way:

> *Class 1—figures have cross-hatching within them.*
> *Class 2—figures contain parallel lines.*
> *Class 3—figures contain right angles.*
> *Class 4—figures are black.*
> *Class 5—figures contain curved lines.*

You would show that you cognized these classes correctly by saying which figure, *A* through *E,* belongs in each class. *B* does not fit any class.

Figure 4.3

Some items for a matching exercise from a *Figure Classification Test.*

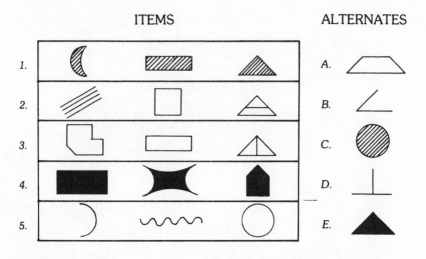

Decide what the nature of each numbered class is, then select the one numbered figure at the right that belongs to the same class.

Symbolic Classes (CSC)

Previously it was shown how classes can be formed of words in terms of their letter contents (see p. 27) Classes can also be formed with numbers, as in the following test items. The task is to decide the nature of the numbered class, then to find among the alternatives at the right the one that fits into the class.

Number-class:			Alternatives:
1. 44 .88 55			A. 421
2. 45 60 15			B. 16
3. 23 35 91			C. 70
4. 64 49 4			D. 22
			E. 14

The answers to these items, with reasons, are:

1. D *(double digits, or multiples of 11)*
2. C *(multiples of 5)*
3. A *(odd numbers)*
4. B *(squares of numbers)*

Semantic Classes (CMC)

In the following lists of four words each, which word does not belong to the same class with the rest? Your answer is expected to show whether or not you cognize the class.

	a	*b*	*c*	*d*
1.	airplane	glider	truck	motorcycle
2.	handsome	blond	distinguished	stoop-shouldered
3.	charitable	relaxed	comfortable	at ease
4.	desert	prairie	turf	valley

The right answers and common features for the classes are:

1. b *(The others are powered vehicles.)*
2. c *(physical characteristics)*
3. a *(physical state)*
4. c *(large areas of land)*

It would be well to mention that there can be classes of things other than units — classes of classes, for example. The terms "dog," "turtle," "deer," and "worm" each can refer to a class, some of whose members you could probably name. All of them belong to the much larger class of animals, parallel to the large class of plants. Both are in the even larger class of "living things." Such a classes-within-classes arrangement is a hierarchy, which is an important model for organizing things that we know. The famous classification of Linnaeus in biology is a classical example. Such a model is a semantic system.

Behavioral Classes (CBC)

As might be expected, a test for *CBC* would involve the use of pictured expressional behavior. This is true of the item in *Figure 4.4*. There the first three expressions are intended to represent a certain class of mental states. The biting of fingernails, playing with a ring on a finger, and sitting tensely with legs curled around chair legs, all point to a tense mental state. Which of the four alternative answers is the best candidate for the same class? It is, of course, the man who is twisting his hair, answer number 2.

Figure 4.4

A sample item from the test *Expression Grouping*.

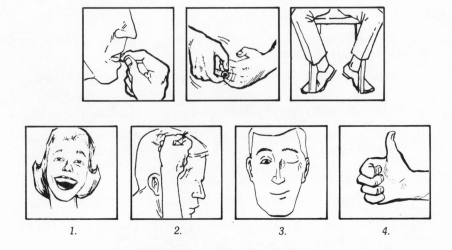

1.   2.   3.   4.

COGNITION OF RELATIONS

Another important way in which to organize information is to see relations between things. The more relations we can see the more relevant and significant they become and therefore the more useful.

Visual Relations (CVR)

The kind of task most often used to assess *CVR* is a figure-analogies test. One form of such a test appears in *Figure 3.1* (p. 29). In *Figure 4.5* are some items from a more complicated task. Three columns and rows are used. A certain relation is repeated within rows and another relation within columns, and some figures are missing. It must be decided what kind of figure should replace each question mark so as to maintain the same relations already seen in the matrix. The right answers for items *1* through *3* are *A*, *B*, and *A*, respectively. A close study of the given items will show why these answers are correct.

Figure 4.5

Sample items from the *Figure Matrix Test.*

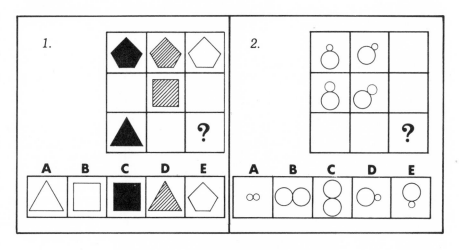

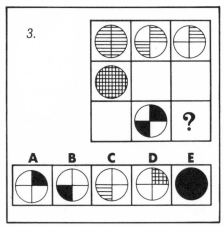

Symbolic Relations (CSR)

Analogies tests are also useful for assessing cognition of relations in the symbolic area, and some examples were given in *Chapter 3* (p. 30). Another kind of task known as a "trend" test has the same relation repeated several times in a series of units. Consider the following items. What is the nature of the trend; what is the relation in each item?

1.	anger	bacteria	camel	dead	excite
2.	rated	crate	morning	dearth	separate
3.	tire	timid	insipid	initiation	divisibility
4.	little	astute	taste	instinct	sentiment

The relations that should be stated to describe the trends in these lists are:

1. *Initial letters in pairs of words are in direct alphabetical order.*
2. *The letter r moves one place to the right in each added word.*
3. *The number of i's increases by one each time.*
4. *The two t's move one more letter apart each time.*

Incidentally, some of these statements read as if they were describing systems rather than relations; they state principles. The end result in each item is actually a system, but one particular relation is the key to the system. The relation could be seen in any one pair of words.

Semantic Relations (CMR)

For *CMR* we can also give a trend test. Here are some sample items:

1. mouse   cat   pig   horse   elephant
         (relation is size)

2. century   decade   year   month   day
         (length of time interval)

3. alert   awake   relaxed   drowsy   asleep
         (degree of wakefulness)

The following task is rather different and probably a little more challenging. It requires seeing two different relations that a given thing may have to two other things. Which of the words, *A* through *C*, in each item, is related in different ways to the two given words?

1. *JEWELRY—BELL*
   A. ornament   B. jingle   C. ring

2. *FOOTBALL—EXAMINATION*
   A. yard   B. pass   C. pad

3. *RADIO—TOOTHPASTE*
   A. tube   B. cap   C. station

4. *WINTER—PEPPER*
   A. *season*   B. *spring*   C. *bell*

5. *BIRD—DOLLAR*
   A. *fly*   B. *buck*   C. *bill*

In case you have not seen all the relations, the answers are: *C, B, A, A,* and *C,* respectively.

Behavioral Relations (CBR)

When two people are interacting face to face, there is likely to be a certain relation between the mental states of the two. In *Figure 4.6* are two individuals facing each other. In order to decide what the relation is between them, we have to consider the expressions on *both* faces. The task is to decide what the person with the arrow beneath him is saying or thinking in connection with the other one. Three alternative answers are given with the two faces. Answer number 1 ignores the other person; it could be said or thought without the presence of the second face. The statement "What a bore" is also consistent with the first face but it ignores the other fellow's angry expression, which should tell us more than that. Both are angry and are perhaps having an argument. Answer 3 is therefore the best one.

Figure 4.6

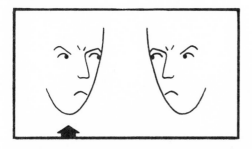

1) I didn't like that movie very much.
2) What a bore!
3) Who does he think he is, anyway?

(From faces originally designed by M. G. Cline.)

COGNITION OF SYSTEMS

Visual Systems (CVS)

Much was said in the preceding chapter about the organized space that we see around us as a visual-figural system. *Figure 3.3* (p. 33) presented one kind of task requiring the perceiving of arrangements of letters on the sides of cubes. Another kind of task for this ability is shown in *Figure 4.7*. It is a little different because it brings the viewer into the problem in relation to the objects in view.

At the left is a picture of four balls arranged in a certain series on the background of a white cross. Photographs were taken of the same arrangement from different directions, as noted by the letters around the circle, *A* through *H*. Three of these pictures are shown in the test items at the right. From which direction was each one taken? The three directions were *E*, *D*, and *A*, which should not be very difficult for anyone with a moderate degree of *CVS* to cognize.

Symbolic Systems (CSS)

In *Chapter 3*, letter series and number series were mentioned as examples of symbolic systems. A different kind of letter system is illustrated in the following items. What two letters should follow in each item to fill in the blank?

1. *A C A B A C A B A* __ __
2. *C A C A B C C A C A* __ __
3. *A A B A C A A B A* __ __

The three correct completions, in order, are: *C A, B C,* and *C A.*

Figure 4.7

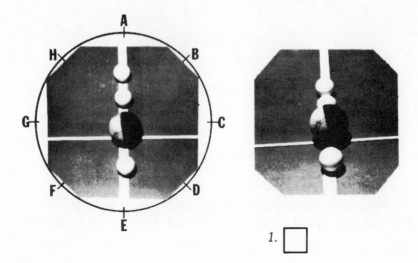

If you have studied algebra you should be prepared to believe that ability *CSS* has some usefulness in that subject, for it calls for the grasping of somewhat complex letter-and-number expressions and equations.

Semantic Systems (CMS)

You saw in *Chapter 3* that an arithmetical problem, verbally conceived, is a good example of a semantic system. Now it can be added that understanding the problem is a matter of *CMS*. If a person solves the problem correctly we know, of course, that he has cognized the system. It was said that another way of knowing just that a problem is understood is to ask the person what fact or facts are lacking in an incomplete statement of the problem. Still another way is to ask what numerical operations are needed in order to solve the problem, all the facts being given. What numerical steps must be applied in order to solve each of these problems?

1. A city lot is 48 feet wide and 149 feet long, and it cost $75,432. What is the cost per square foot?

2. A tree casts a shadow 12 feet long at the same time that a five-foot vertical pole casts a shadow 2 feet long. What is the height of the tree?

3. Bob Jones receives pay of $800 a month. He spends $185 for rent, $200 for food, and $300 for other expenses. How much money does he save in a year?

2. ☐   3. ☐

It should not be very difficult to see what operations should be done. They are: *(1) multiply and divide; (2) divide and multiply;* and *(3) add, subtract, and multiply.*

It is reasonable to find that *CMS* is important at any level of mathematics where problems are thought out in terms of concepts. One can also imagine the usefulness of this ability to the detective, who must organize his facts into a pattern that describes the crime and thus points to suspects. This activity would take him also into the behavioral area, which comes next.

Behavioral Systems (CBS)

The series of pictures at the top of *Figure 4.8* tells a story. One of the four pictures is missing, and the series is to be completed by inserting one of the pictures from the bottom three. Which one of the three makes the most reasonable story, especially considering the attitude of the girl in the fourth picture? Number 2 would make the best sense. The blonde is evidently telling the brunette something about the man and it is not pleasant news to the brunette.

Can you walk into a room in which several people are interacting, and quickly size up the situation? If you can, you probably rank at least fair in ability *CBS.* On such occasions this ability should help you in giving close attention to pairs of people, seeing relations, and then linking your observations together. As with other intellectual abilities, practice should pay off in terms of grasping behavioral systems.

COGNITION OF TRANSFORMATIONS

As said before *(Chapter 3),* transformations may be observed while they are happening or we can know that they take place from what we see before and after. In either case, we are cognizing transformations.

Visual Transformations (CVT)

At some time you have probably performed the act of paper folding and cutting. There is a paper-cutting-and-folding test, from which three items are given in *Figure 4.9.* Each item starts with two drawings. In the first one there is one fold. The dotted line shows the outline before the folded part had been turned. The second drawing shows two operations —a second fold, and, in black, the portion that has been cut out. If the paper were then unfolded, which figure below would show how it will look, including the creases and holes? The answers for the three items are: *C, D,* and *B.*

Figure 4.8

?

Ability *CVT* is known to be important for students in courses in drafting and engineering drawing, as well as in courses in higher mathematics. It should also be useful to the inventor of mechanical devices with moving parts as well as to the operators and repairmen of those devices.

Symbolic Transformations (CST)

Two examples of tests for this ability were given in the preceding chapter, one involving reading backwards and the other involving

Figure 4.9

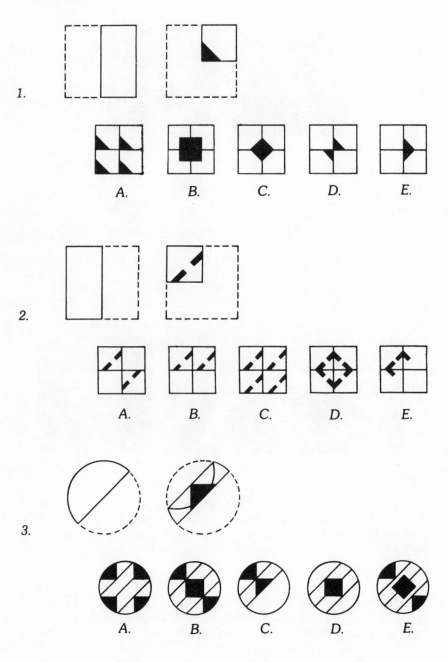

transposed letters in spoonerisms. In a third test presented here, you are asked to tell what changes have been made in the spelling of a word when it is given twice, as in the following items:

1. *ingenuous - ingenious*   *(u changed to i)*
2. *equipment - equiptment*   *(t added)*
3. *apperceive - appercieve*   *(e and i interchanged)*
4. *judgment - judgement*   *(e added)*

Such an exercise is found in the performance of a proofreader who compares one copy of printed material with another. Just identifying words that have been misspelled as they appear alone, however, is a matter of ability *CSU*. In the items just given, you would not have to know the correct spelling of words; both words could be misspelled.

Semantic Transformations (CMT)

You have already seen that a common example of a semantic transformation is a pun. In a test called *Daffynitions,* you are to see some puns based upon given words. In response to each word, you are to "Say something clever," which invites puns. Examples have been given. Suppose the given words were: *TREE, DECIDE, SINK,* and *ADDRESS.* Sound the words to yourself and see what similar words with other meanings come to mind. Here are some responses that have been given to the words:

TREE   *I have tree pencils.*
DECIDE   *De side of de barn is red.*
SINK   *I don't sink so.*
ADDRESS   *Address is beautiful.*

In a less humorous vein, another test asks you to tell what different meanings you can think of for a common ambiguous word. Take the word "case," for example. It might mean suit case, case in court, case of mumps, or just in case. Now try yourself on three other words: *BAR, CAST,* and *ORDER.*

It has been demonstrated that seeing semantic transformations is important in the learning of new facts from reading. Students were given short essays to read, after which their memory for the facts was tested. It was found that a good score in the memory test depended in part upon ability *CMT.* The reason probably is that in reading for new information, the student must make some revisions in what he already knows. This step tends to increase his attention, which is favorable for cognition and memory. As you read new material it would be quite beneficial to make revisions in what you know and to take note of those changes.

Behavioral Transformations (CBT)

Becoming aware of a change in the role of a certain bit of behavior is illustrated in *Figure 4.10*. The man at the top right is holding his nose for a reason indicated by the expression of the face at the left. The question is, which man in the group below would hold his nose but for a different reason? Man number *1* would seem to have no reason to be holding his nose. Number *2* might do so, but it could be for the same reason as for the man on the left. Number *3*, who is inflating his cheeks by forcing air into them, would be likely to hold his nose in order to prevent leaking air, so *3* is the right answer.

Figure 4.10

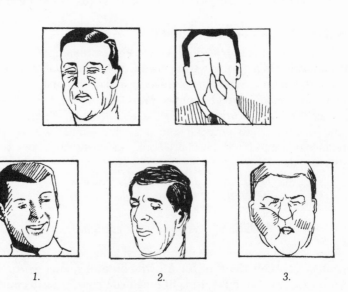

1.   2.   3.

COGNITION OF IMPLICATIONS

Implications enable us to see beyond the things immediately observed or given, whatever the kind of information. It has already been stated that implications are extensions, things expected, or things suggested by what is given. By this process our ability to gain new information is greatly extended.

Visual Implications (CVI)

You saw in *Figure 3.5* (p. 41) some instances of how given figures can be extended, some to the point of natural completions. In *Figure 4.11* there is a different kind of exercise for *CVI*. The task is to identify through which lettered point the line would pass if the arc were extended to form a complete circle. In the two items given, the circles would pass through points *D* and *B*.

Figure 4.11

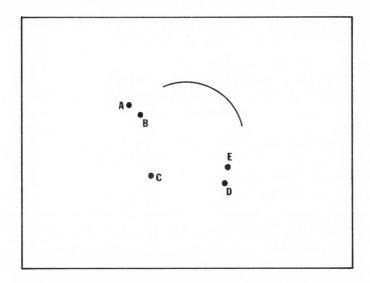

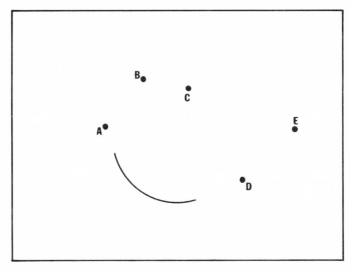

With a little consideration, you should be able to think of examples of visual implications in daily life. If you want to reach an object that is above your outstretched fingertips, you think of something of about the right height on which to stand. The world of sports offers numerous instances of visual implication. In driving an automobile, you need to predict where other cars will be at a given short time ahead so as to make the appropriate responses, to avoid collisions, and to achieve certain goals. In a game of chess or checkers you do best by anticipating your opponent's moves.

Symbolic Implications (CSI)

In the preceding chapter you saw samples of activities that call for seeing implications from symbolic information. No further examples should be needed in the form of test items here. Ability *CSI* has naturally been found important in the study of algebra, where expressions and equations imply others.

Semantic Implications (CMI)

Seeing meaningful implications is a very widely useful ability. One of the most important roles for *CMI* is in seeing that problems exist. One cannot begin to solve problems by ignoring them or being oblivious to them.

What problems might arise in connection with the following objects: a candle, a tree, an automobile, or a telephone? For the candle you might ask how to take care of its drippings; how to prevent it from starting fires; how to make it stand without a holder; or where to keep it so you can find it when you need it. For the tree you could ask: where to plant it to give the shade you want; how to select it for the size you want when it is grown; and how and when to fertilize it. You have no doubt had enough experiences with automobiles and telephones to know of problems arising from those devices. Every problem you give is suggested by the nature of the object, particularly its shortcomings.

Asking questions is an art and a skill that should and can be developed. It may help in its development to know that a question is a semantic implication from a given object or situation. Questions lead to problem solving and perhaps to invention or innovation, hence creative production. Questions beginning with "Why can't we . . . ?" are particularly conducive to such thinking. It is often said that "Necessity is the mother of invention." Here are a few needs that have been expressed: to be able to use a credit card in a pay telephone; a vacuum cleaner that guides itself around the room; an "alarm bed" that brings the sleeper to a sitting position at the desired moment; snow tires with retractable knobs; and an extension cord that retracts into the wall when it is not needed. If you want to be creative, look around you for new needs. This is the way to start.

Behavioral Implications (CBI)

One way of testing for ability *CBI* is to present action pictures, as in a cartoon, with the examinee to tell what should come next. In *Figure 4.12* we see in the first section a man named "Barney" hanging dangerously from an eave trough. His little son is looking on evidently in some surprise if not dismay. Picture number *1* is the most likely prediction, for the boy has told his mother and she has brought a ladder to rescue Barney. From Barney's look of fear and despair in the first picture, it is not likely that he engages in an active and strenuous effort to climb up on the roof. From the look of concern of the boy in the first picture, it is not likely that he and his mother will simply laugh at Barney, as in picture number *3*.

No one can deny the value of being able to predict what people will do next. What you do or say may be aimed at having certain effects on the other fellow. Before you take an action it is a good idea to think what the probable effects will be on others. Success in all these respects depends upon ability *CBI*.

COGNITION AND LEARNING

By now it should be clear that cognition has a lot to do with learning. Although it is true that as you try to do most of the illustrative test items the task is largely a matter of re-cognition. You have solved the same problems or something similar in your previous experience. But recognition is still cognition, for which we have more or less preparation from the past. There is a first time for the emergence of any item of information, a moment of discovery when a new product or construct is formed. Otherwise, it is a matter of rediscovery or relearning.

What can we learn from this parade of cognition abilities regarding ways to aid learning in general? First, it may help to realize that the thing to be learned is a certain kind of product in a certain content area. This step would narrow the goal somewhat; seeing what kind of information you need and do not have. The search could be narrowed a little further by being aware of the class within which the needed product lies. This tactic points to the importance of having in your memory store a good supply of class ideas to use in this connection.

Beyond this bit of advice some general rules can be stated:

1. *Be a good observer.* Pay close attention to all signif-

Figure 4.12

icant aspects of input information. What are its properties or attributes? In other words, what are its classes?

2. *Be a good organizer.* Besides organizing your information in classes, look for relations between items. Relations provide useful ties, making information more useful. Go further by organizing systems, another way of making information meaningful and significant.

3. *Be a good transformer.* But do not let your organized items become too rigid. Be ready to modify them if need be and if you see needs for improvement. Remember the earlier statement about the role of transformations in learning and remembering facts.

4. *Be a good deducer.* By this is meant to look for implications to information that you encounter. Ask questions about it. Make predictions about it. See where it fits into the general scheme of things. Application of these rules should make learning not only easier but also more rewarding.

SUMMARY

From the kinds of things that the illustrative problems in this chapter require you to do, you can see what events occur under the heading of cognition. Among other things you were asked to identify objects, words, meanings, and mental states of persons, all of which are units of information. You were asked to recognize classes in which things belong, sets of visual figures with attributes in common, also sets of numbers, for example. Some problems asked you to see how two things are related, such as two ideas or two facial expressions. Relations were also presented in the form of trends, in which things vary along certain dimensions.

In other problems you were asked to see rules, principles, or orders, and arrangements or organizations of elements; in other words, systems. Some test items involved awareness of changes of various kinds — movements or other changes in objects that you see, in the spelling of words, in the use of familiar objects, or in the interpretation of someone's behavior. All these items are transformations. Cognition of implications takes various forms: predicting where lines will go if extended, extensions of letter patterns, or what a person will do next. Our knowledge is perpetually going beyond what is immediately given.

Cognition involves the act of structuring information. For any item of information there is always a first time for it to emerge as a construct. This is learning. In the understanding and control of learning, it should be important to know about the ways in which products of information are formed, in any kind of content.

CHAPTER FIVE

Putting Information Into Storage: Memory

No one should doubt the value of having a good memory store, for what is in that store contributes to all the different mental operations. The ancient Greeks valued memory so highly that they assigned a special goddess to it by the name of Mnemosyne. In our present-day civilization we find not only an abundance of articles and books on the topic, but also a willingness of people to subscribe to courses on how to improve memory.

We are concerned here with how information in its various forms is put into memory storage. This is a step in the chain of mental events over which we know we can exert some control. It helps us to know about the memorizing of different forms of information, for every kind presents somewhat different problems. The kinds and forms are those in the categories of information as presented in the matrix of *Chapter 3*. There is nothing to say as yet regarding memory for auditory or behavioral information, for those areas of memory abilities have not yet been investigated.

The modern psychology of memory recognizes two major kinds of memory. In short-term memory information is held at a usable level for a matter of seconds; a few minutes at the most. On the exact time limit there is no universal agreement. Long-term memory is believed to depend upon the formation of new protein molecules, or structures composed of molecules, in the brain, and this takes a little time.

There is evidence for a set of short-term memory abilities and a parallel set of long-term memory abilities. The latter are somewhat dependent upon the former because obviously if we do not remember something over the short term it is unlikely that we remember it over the long term. The two sets of abilities are parallel, so what is described in the following pages should apply to both.

Figure 5.1

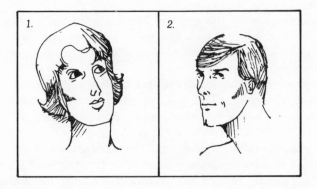

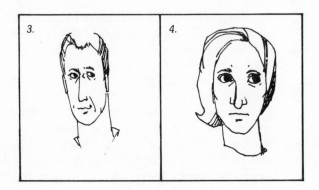

MEMORY FOR UNITS

Visual Units (MVU)

How well can you remember faces — just from their appearances — so that you can recognize them when you see them again? A test has been developed for this particular kind of exercise. On a study page are ten different faces, like the top pair in *Figure 5.1,* five male and five female. The examinee studies the ten faces for two minutes then turns to a test page. On this page the same ten faces are given again, but scrambled among ten new ones not seen by the examinee before. He is to identify the ones he had seen.

What can we tell the person who wants to improve his memory for what he sees — faces in particular? One important principle to know about is that the memory impression of information decays with time, as we all have found. It loses its distinctness; its differentiation from other information. Outlines become blurred and uncertain; details drop out; attributes are lost. In cognizing the item of information it is therefore important to sharpen the impression of it as much as possible.

When you wish to remember a person's face, it is important to take note of its various attributes, especially those that are rare, even unique. Note its general shape, size, skin color, and texture; its kinds of hair, eyes, eyebrows, nose, mouth, and chin. The survey can be very rapid; the characteristics taken in very quickly. Each face is a unique pattern of attributes. The most difficult kind of face to recognize is one belonging to a type; it looks like a lot of other faces. For such persons we need to look for at least one unique sign, such as a mole or a dimple.

Symbolic Units (MSU)

You would expect that memory for symbolic information should be tested by using letters or numbers. Meaningful words would not be good for this purpose because of their double nature. They could be learned as either symbolic or semantic information, or both. For symbolic units a popular item of information has been the nonsense syllable; a three-letter unit that stands for nothing familiar, like *PUM* or *MIJ*.

Like the *Memory-for-Faces* test just used for *MVU,* we can give a memory task that calls for the recognition of nonsense syllables, as shown below:

From the study page:	*From the test page:*
GAJ	1. COF
COF	2. SIJ
MIW	3. GAJ
FEQ	4. MOZ

Having studied a list of 15 syllables on the study page, the examinee later says which ones among 30 he tried to memorize.

The recognition of words just from their spelling is, of course, one of the essential activities in learning to read. It usually takes more than one exposure before a letter combination that forms a word becomes familiar. With real words the child can take advantage of pronunciation, and thus reinforce his memory through his auditory channel and auditory-figural information. Pronounceable nonsense syllables are also more easily remembered. Thus, some auditory memory may be involved in the syllable test just illustrated.

Semantic Units (MMU)

MMU means memory for meanings, apart from any word labels. In a test for *MMU*, therefore, in order to be sure that it is memory for meaning only, we need to give certain words that have well-recognized meaning to be studied. In testing memory for meaning only, we present synonyms of those words, mixed with new words. Here are a few examples:

From the study page:	*From the test page:*	
LAMP	1. *toaster*	4. *lantern*
TO SEARCH	2. *brave*	5. *to hunt*
COURAGEOUS	3. *to write*	6. *shy*

The examinee should, of course, say *Yes* to items 2, 4, and 5.

A somewhat different type of test that requires *recall* of information rather than recognition is illustrated in *Figure 5.2*. On a study page are pictured 20 familiar objects that probably everyone knows by sight. On a test page the examinee is to write the names of as many objects as he can remember.

Figure 5.2

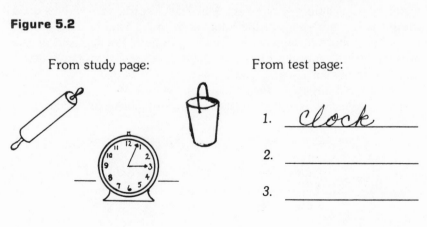

From study page: From test page:

1. *Clock*

2. _____

3. _____

One of the places in daily life in which memory for objects is of considerable importance is on the witness stand in a criminal trial. The witness may be called upon to say whether the suspect had a gun or a knife; whether he wore a jacket or a sweater; whether he struck the victim or tried to choke him; whether anyone else was present, and so on. These are all isolated facts or semantic units. A popular demonstration in some psychology or law classes has been to have a couple of characters break into the room and stage a "crime" lasting a matter of seconds. When it is over, the class is asked to write an account of what happened. Differences between reports is sometimes amazing. Memory may actually have been good but many cognitions go astray.

MEMORY FOR CLASSES

Because the classes in our mental equipment are so important in remembering units, it is also important that we put classes into storage. Classes are very much needed in retrieving information that we need to use. You have probably had experiences like the following:

> You encounter a need to recall a certain person's name that does not come immediately to mind. You first think "The person's name begins with M." That puts it in a very broad class; not much help, but a start in narrowing the field. Then you think it ends in "n"; in fact, the ending is "son." The class is now even smaller. Then you recall that it has a "t" in it, then, with a flash, the name "Mortonson" comes to mind, and you have arrived!

This is an illustration of retrieval of symbolic information; the same principle applies in other areas.

Visual Classes (MVC)

Figure 5.3 shows examples of items from a recognition test for MVC. On the study page are sets of three figures each, each set belonging to a particular figural class. In the two sets shown there, one is of simple angles and the other is of simple, incomplete figures; figures with gaps in them. On the test page each item presents a single figure, and you are to remember whether it belongs to any class that you saw on the study page. Items 2 and 3 belong in the two classes whereas 1 and 4 do not. You would, of course, have to decide the answers *Yes* or *No* without having the class sets in view.

Figure 5.3

Two classes from the study page:

Four figures from the test page:

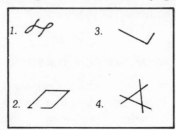

Symbolic Classes (MSC)

A recognition test for *MSC* presents three-word sets of real words that form classes in terms of their letter content, not in terms of meaning, as in the following samples:

Sample sets from the study page:

ran	test	jump
pan	pest	jury
fan	lest	just

Sample items from the test page:

1. west   4. pin
2. boat   5. lure
3. can   6. June

Words in items *1, 3,* and *6* belong to classes to be memorized; the others do not.

A recall test for *MSC* uses classes of numbers. Number sets of three numbers each are given for study, for example: *10, 5, 25; 307, 602, 740;* and *621, 821, 221.* Having studied a longer list, you would turn the page and write down what number classes you had seen. For the three number sets just given you would say *multiples of five, contain a zero,* and *end in 21,* respectively.

Semantic Classes (MMC)

Tests for *MMC* would naturally group meanings. Presentations can be either in terms of words or pictures of common objects. One that uses words is like the following material:

Sample sets from a study page:

<u>*a*</u>	<u>*b*</u>
silk	violet
wool	aster
nylon	pansy

Sample items from a test page:

1.	2.	3.	4.
snow	satin	rose	wall
ice	felt	poppy	window
sleet	cotton	tulip	floor

Which classes from the test page are the same as the two classes seen on the study page? The classes of clothing material *(2)* and of flowers *(3)* should be easy to find if one happens to remember having seen them on the study page.

MEMORY FOR RELATIONS

Visual Relations (MVR)

You have already seen that where relations are concerned we can use tests composed of analogies or of trends. The illustration for a trend-memory test is given in *Figure 5.4*. In each row of squares on a study page a certain relation is seen repeated from one square to the next. The first row shows the addition of one dot and the second row shows decreasing amounts of blackened space. Repeating rows of squares on the test page would make the test also a measure of *MVU*, so the relations are transposed to circles on the test page to help minimize this diversion.

Symbolic Relations (MSR)

One test for *MSR* uses names of people, and the relation in each case is between the first and second name. The following examples will illustrate this:

Names from a study page:

Sam Martin	Robert Redding
Tom McTavish	Rose Reardon
Pam Morton	Roxana Reed

Items from a test page:

1. Roberta	2. Tim
A. Rollins	A. Thompson
B. Revere	B. Traver
C. Radford	C. Manson
D. Baller	D. Tolman

It will be noted that the repeated relation in the first column from the study page is that the end letter of the first name is the same as the initial letter of the second name. In the second column, the first name begins with *Ro* and the second with *Re. B* and *C* are the correct answers.

Semantic Relations (MMR)

For a sample test for *MMR,* let us take one of a still different type. In the *Remembered Relations* test the examinee is told what the relation is

Figure 5.4

In the test *Remembering Figural Trends,* you would need to see and memorize the relation in each series of squares in order later to recognize it in series of circles.

From the study page:

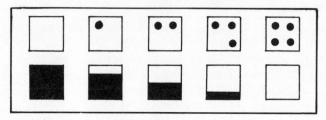

From the test page:

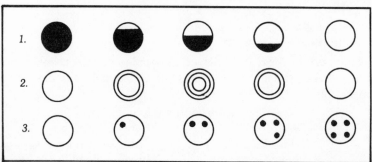

on the study page, as in the sentence *Diamonds are harder than coal.*
Found on the test page is an item for this particular relation, reading:

Coal is _____ *than diamonds.*

A. *softer*   B. *blacker*   C. *less valuable*   D. *dirtier*

Note that the direction of the relation is reversed in the test item, in
order to help concentrate on the relation itself. The same wording as on
the study page is thus avoided. Note, also, that the alternative answers
are all valid relations that would satisfy the statement. However, of all the
relations given in the test item, only one was mentioned on the study
page, although in reverse.

MEMORY FOR SYSTEMS

Visual Systems (MVS)

Remember that as informational products systems are arrangements or patterns of elements. In testing memory for systems, as such,
then, it is retention of *arrangements* in which we are interested. On the
test page we might supply the examinee with all the elements and ask
him to arrange them as he had seen them on the study page. This is the
principle used in a test called *Monogram Recall.*

A monogram for a person's name, of course, is an interesting,
perhaps even artistic, arrangement of intial letters. On the study page in
Monogram Recall are given five different arrangements of the three
letters, as in the first row of *Figure 5.5,* with three monograms. On the
test page the three letters only are given and the examinee is to try to
reconstruct the arrangements that he had seen.

Figure 5.5

Some study-page monograms:

Given on the test page:

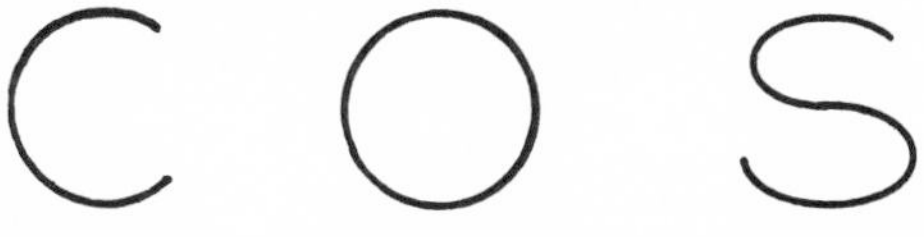

Symbolic Systems (MSS)

A very old, favorite type of test for memory is known as a *Memory-Span* test. Either a digit-span or a letter-span test would do. In either case, in each item the examiner reads aloud (or presents visually, it does not matter which) a list of digits or of letters, one at a time, just once, and you are to reproduce the list, all in the right order. It is the requirement of *in the right order* that makes the list a system. The lists vary in length, as in the following set:

$$8 \quad 4 \quad 1 \quad 6 \quad 9$$
$$3 \quad 2 \quad 9 \quad 7 \quad 6 \quad 8$$
$$5 \quad 4 \quad 8 \quad 1 \quad 3 \quad 7 \quad 9$$
$$4 \quad 6 \quad 1 \quad 7 \quad 9 \quad 3 \quad 5 \quad 2$$
$$2 \quad 5 \quad 8 \quad 1 \quad 3 \quad 7 \quad 4 \quad 9 \quad 6$$

Other sets of lists would also be administered in order to make the test more accurate. The average college student can recite correctly a series of seven digits in half the time that a series of that length is presented.

People who have practiced on a memory-span task can increase their spans up to 12 or more digits. One of the useful tactics in doing this is to group the digits, another is to introduce a rhythm into the series, and still another is to give greater attention to the digits in the middle part of the series, because those digits tend to be forgotten first. A seven-digit telephone number is rather taxing for most people, even though it is divided. How often have you started confidently to dial a number and forget part of it before you have finished dialing? The best remedy for this, of course, is to repeat the whole number to yourself a few times before starting to dial it.

Memory span is related to the age of the individual as development occurs. This is one reason why it is tested at various ages in the *Stanford-Binet Scale*. The child is given three trials at each length of series and is said to have reached a certain mental-age level if he recites two series out of three correctly for that age standard. The age standards are approximately as follows:

Digits	3	4	5	6	7
Age	4	6	9	12	16

Semantic Systems (MMS)

Another type of test in the semantic area shows more clearly that we are dealing with order of elements. In *Memory for Events*, an *MMS* test, the elements are stated events or actions and the test of retention is a quiz concerning order within the series. The events are listed in order on the study page but listed in pairs for items on the test page, with the examineee to say which event of each pair happened earlier.

Sample list from the study page:
While in the park, Joan:
   rode on the carousel
   fed the monkeys
   ate an ice-cream cone
   sat on a park bench
   played a dart game

Sample items: Which came first?
1. A. *sat on a park bench*
   B. *rode on the carousel*
2. A. *fed the monkeys*
   B. *played a dart game*
3. A. *sat on a park bench*
   B. *ate an ice-cream cone*

This test suggests that MMS is likely to be involved in remembering sequences of personal events occurring over longer periods of time, and also remembering the order of historical events. Daily routines, organizational features of a business firm or a political jurisdiction, and plans for a program, all are systems and must be remembered as well as comprehended by many people who are involved.

MEMORY FOR TRANSFORMATIONS

Visual Transformations (MVT)

In tests for MVT you would expect to see some changes of certain kinds on a study page and to be tested for memory of those changes later. *Figure 5.6* shows one kind of test in this category. Given a set of solid objects of certain shapes and positions, you are to imagine each object being turned so that its front, which is labeled, would be directly toward you and at eye level. On the test page you are called upon to recognize the front views you should have imagined. This activity involves memory for the transformation itself. In the illustrative test items, answers 1 and 4 should be recognized, 2 and 3 not.

MVT should play a role in a number of dealings with concrete materials and problems. Memory of how a mechanical puzzle was solved would be one example. An inventor's solution to a new problem should be facilitated by remembering what happened to moving parts on previous occasions. Athletes should benefit from having a good memory store of movements that they observed as they practiced their skills.

Figure 5.6

From study page:

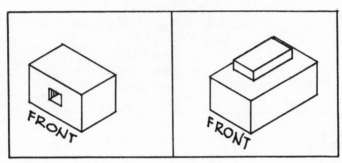

From test page:

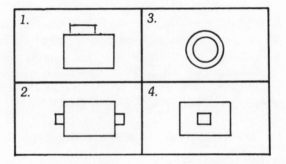

Symbolic Transformations (MST)

One interesting test for *MST* is *Memory for Misspellings*. A misspelling is a transformation. On a study page is given a list of very familiar words that are misspelled. The misspellings are phonetic, so the words should be readily recognized. On a test page the same words are listed but correctly spelled. The examinee is supposed to tell how each word was misspelled. Some examples follow:

Misspelled words on a study page:	From a test page: How were these words misspelled?
boan	1. girl
ketle	2. bone
fasen	3. fasten
girll	4. kettle
anjel	5. angel

One area in school work in which this kind of transformation is important is mathematics. In learning how to factor expressions or to revise equations in algebra, one has to learn several standard transformations. With these items of information in storage, the student is ready to face future operations in mathematics.

Semantic Transformations (MMT)

In discussing semantic transformations earlier, the pun was mentioned more than once as an example. Puns have also been used in testing for *MMT*. In the test *Remembering Puns,* a study page gives a list of sentences, in each of which are one or two pun words. These words are underlined to show the location of the puns. We have to assume that the examinee cognizes the transformation in seeing the pun, for if he does not, there is no chance of his storing it in memory. In the recall test, each pun word is given in an item, with the examinee to write the word of the other meaning. For example, take this sentence from the study page:

> College <u>bred</u> means a four-year <u>loaf</u> made from the old
> man's <u>dough.</u>

On the test page we find the items:

> 1. BRED - _____ and 2. DOUGH - _____

The examinee should, of course, write *bread* and *money* in the two blanks.

Another test uses homonyms — words sounding the same but spelled and meaning differently. Pairs of such words are presented for study, of which the following is an example:

> There is a <u>hole</u> in the wall.
> He ate the <u>whole</u> pie.

The item on the test page that assesses retention of this transformation of meaning reads:

> ENTIRE   A. nut   B. ship   C. opening   D. operation

The task in this item is to find among the alternatives the word that should be paired with the word *ENTIRE,* which is, of course, *C.* Both words are synonyms of the paired homonyms on the study page.

In *Chapter 4* it was pointed out that the corresponding ability *CMT* is of value in learning new facts from reading. It was found in the same study that the memory ability *MMT* also makes a contribution to remembering the facts. If a fact had to be revised, remembering that revision seems to help remember the fact on which the examinees were tested. So, as you read, be on the lookout for transformations and try to remember them.

MEMORY FOR IMPLICATIONS

If you will remember, an implication involves two things. The one implies or suggests the other. An implication is a kind of connection between two items, so that one leads you to expect the other, or from one of them you predict the other. It is the connection that must be learned and put in storage.

Visual Implications (MVI)

A task for assessing ability *MVI* is called *Face-Shield Matching*. In it you have to learn and store connections between faces and shields with family crests. *Figure 5.7* shows some sample faces with their accompanying shields. They are paired off on the study page. Later they are all presented again, but scrambled, and you have to tell which shield goes with each face. A matching test is ideal for this kind of ability because it tests memory for implications only, and not for units or relations, except as some examinees invent their own relations.

This ability should be relevant for producers in the various visual arts and for those who invent mechanical things. They would do well to stockpile in memory storage items of information that naturally go together.

Symbolic Implications (MSI)

The matching type of test can also be usefully applied with symbolic information, pairing off letters, syllables, or numbers. The illustration of an *MSI* test given here pairs persons' family names with their initials, as in the following abbreviated test:

From the study page:	From the test page:	
J. M. Fox	1. Cramer	W. E. _____
W. E. Phelps	2. Wells	J. M. _____
T. N. Wells	3. Fox	A. V. _____
A. V. Cramer	4. Phelps	T. N. _____

Secretaries, clerks, and others often have problems similar to the one just illustrated. *MSI* is also important in any tasks that involve numerical operations, although the advent of the vest-pocket calculator seems to be rapidly downgrading that importance. But there are still numerous tasks around that call for the remembering of paired labels of one kind or another to speak for its value.

Figure 5.7

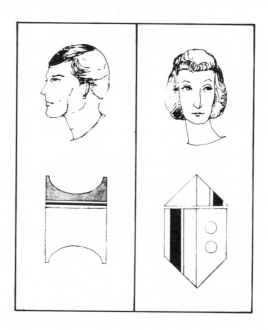

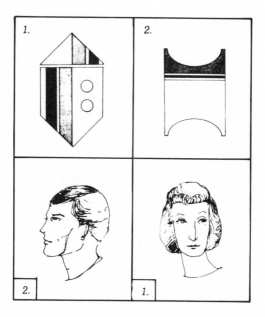

Semantic Implications (MMI)

Meaningful items of information are also connected in pairs, of course, and such connections are encountered by all of us much of the time. We experience numerous objects and events together and remember them together. They come to belong to each other. Cause-and-effect relationships develop. We find that if we do one thing, another is likely to occur.

In one test activity involving *MMI,* pairs of terms are presented on the study page, with each pair containing a person's name and his occupation, such as:

> *Pairs from the study page:*
> *SMITH — bricklayer*
> *JONES — radio announcer*

> *Items from the test page:*

JONES —	SMITH —
A. *watch*	A. *piano*
B. *tire*	B. *microphone*
C. *brick*	C. *typewriter*
D. *microphone*	D. *brick*

Quality of retention is tested regarding each pair by an item that gives the name of the person and several alternative answers. The answers are not names of occupations but are names of objects commonly used in the occupations; they are clearly implied by the occupations or represent them. In part, this plan is to avoid a possible association of the two terms, as symbols. It should be noted, also, that a right answer to one item, like *microphone,* is a wrong answer to some other item. To this extent it is partly a matching test. Although the first terms of pairs are names of persons (just labels) the thing implied in each case is meaningful, and hence semantic. It is the content category of the thing implied that determines the content area of the ability.

SOME GENERAL TIPS ON IMPROVING YOUR MEMORY

Although it isn't feasible at this point to give a complete course on how to manage and improve the memory, it would be a good idea for all of us to take advantage of things that have been learned from the memory abilities. Some more specific suggestions have already been given in connection with particular abilities.

The general rules that follow should be helpful. From what you have seen of the various kinds of memory, you may be able to think of still others.

• Obtain a good cognition.

Some advice given in connection with visual memory for units comes under this rule, which applies quite generally. You can remember only what you have cognized, so you should start with good, clear impressions. Sometimes a person's memory is blamed for his failure to recognize or recall something, when the actual blame belongs to poor cognition. This is particularly true in elderly people who are often said to be forgetful. For them, it is likely that the powers for taking inputs and making something out of them wanes more rapidly than the power to put information into storage or to hold it there.

As suggested before, you achieve a good cognition by observing carefully both general and specific features, giving special attention to unusual or unique distinguishing marks. Remember that information is discrimination, and the way to avoid information from becoming vague and confused with other items is to put sharpened impressions into storage.

• Give good attention to what is to be stored.

This rule is closely connected with the first one, and, when followed, leads to good cognitions. In the lower part of the brain there is a place through which most nervous impulses go. It is known as the "reticular formation." It serves as a kind of valve or gate or filtering device, which lets some nervous signals through and inhibits others. In order to produce most cognitions, the input must arrive at your cerebral cortex. Your filter will serve you best if you let it be flexible so that attention is not glued to only one part of the input but rather is allowed to roam or scan. The reason is that at any one moment the channel for input to your cortex is limited. So you must allow a sort of scanning to take place; the spotlight of attention must be turned rapidly in different directions.

• Translate to another code.

Items of information in the different content categories are not equally easy to put into storage. For most people, symbolic information is probably the most difficult to memorize. We have to make allowances, however. There may be some people for whom symbolic information is the easiest to store. In general, probably the easiest kind for most people to store is semantic, with visual-figural somewhere in between. But, again, there are probably individuals for whom the rank order of difficulty of memorizing is not the one given.

At any rate, the important inference is that a person should try to find out what kind of information is easiest for him in memorizing. If it is semantic, it would be helpful to translate other kinds of information into the semantic category. The possibilities for translation were discussed in *Chapter 2.*

As an example of translation in memorizing, suppose the thing to be learned is a list of nonsense syllables, such as *FID, JUP, MON, DAR, LUC,* and *VIS.* You could translate this series into meaningful words to give: *Fido jumped Monday during Lucy's visit.* This translation is even more helpful because it forms a meaningful sentence, a semantic system. The translation involves some symbolic transformations, as in going from *JUP* to jump and from *DAR* to during. These changes would have to be remembered also, but as was pointed out earlier, transformations seem to help memorizing other products of information. In general, it has been proven that the more meaning we can inject into nonsense syllables, the more readily they can be learned and remembered.

While we are on the subject of translations in memorizing, we should consider more shifts into visual form. The ancient orators were said to have associated each part of a speech with a certain room in a house. Recalling the parts in order was then facilitated by imagining walking from room to room. Some orators imagined parts of the speech written on the walls of rooms.

Resort to visual memory is probably most useful in memory for systems, which can be laid out for visual inspection. Some well-known examples of representing semantic information in visual terms are organizational charts and planned operations. The interrelationships are laid out for visual inspection and visual memory.

● **Memorize in more than one language or code.**

Translation substitutes one code for another. It is possible to translate and yet commit the information to memory storage in both languages. This should increase the chance of retention in at least one of the codes.

● **Attach cues to information.**

In order to retrieve an item of information from memory storage, it is almost necessary to have a cue of some kind that helps to locate the item wanted. The cue implies the item. It serves as a tag or label. It is like a call number that you use in finding a book in a library.

Earlier in this chapter much was said about the importance of organizing information for the sake of good storage. The benefits of organization are seen especially at the time of retrieval or recall, for organization provides cues, which lead to implications. Thus, in learning new material, try to see all the useful implications that you can. Even better, if possible, see relations, or invent them.

- **Make good use of classes.**

In discussing memory for classes it was pointed out that those products are important in connection with retrieval of units. This usefulness goes further. It also applies to classes of systems, relations, or transformations, as well as classes of units.

A typical example could be taken from the process of problem solving. If we can drive a certain car 135 miles on 9 gallons of gasoline under normal conditions, how far could we drive it on 12 gallons? The understanding of the problem is a semantic system. We may recognize it as a familiar *type* of problem that calls for a standard set of operations in order to solve it.

For another example, take a case from medical diagnosis. The patient displays a pattern of symptoms that suggests certain classes of disorders, which the doctor recalls one by one. In order to narrow the class it is necessary to make some medical tests. In general, if we put our problem within a class of problems, we are pointed in the direction of a solution. Classes of solutions are similarly utilized. We shall see much more about solving problems in the chapters that follow.

SUMMARY

According to the view adopted in this book, memory is the unique operation concerned with putting information into memory storage; nothing more. There must be a clear distinction made between the *operation* of memory and the results of that operation, the *memory store*. Retrieving or recalling information from storage involves still other operations that are treated in the next two chapters.

Information is stored in the form in which it was cognized. As in cognition, there are probably at least as many memory abilities as there are kinds of information, in other words, abilities for 30 kinds of information described in *Chapter 3*. Eighteen of these abilities were illustrated by means of tests that are used to assess them.

Each kind of memory, each memory ability, offers its own kind of problems and requirements for memorizing. A knowledge of those abilities suggests a number of specific and general rules for more efficient memory operations.

CHAPTER SIX

Broad Search: Divergent Production

The value of stored information lies in its future usefulness. To be useful when we want it, an item of information must be retrieved from storage. That is what this chapter and the next are about; that is, how we search our memory stores and how we find the item or items that we want. Many different abilities are involved. One set of them applies to broad searches, in which we want to find alternative ideas, all of which satisfy a somewhat general requirement.

Suppose you are in the process of writing a paper and you want a better word than the one you think of first. You then engage in a search among your supply of words that mean about the same until you find one that seems best for the purpose. This is an example of *divergent production*. With sufficient relaxation of your requirement, a number of words will come, among which better ones may be found.

Other search abilities are concerned with satisfying a very restricted requirement; there is only one right answer. The search is focused rather than broad-ranging. For example, if the question is: *What is the capital city of New York?* you might think first of several names of capital cities but only *Albany* satisfies the purpose. Abilities for this kind of activity are concerned with the operation of *convergent production*.

In this chapter we are concerned with the first of these two sets of abilities. The "production" part of the two operation names refers to the fact that you must *produce* or generate an answer; it is not given to you. You may recall from *Chapter 4* that in the typical test of a cognition ability alternative answers are given to the examinee, as in a multiple-choice item, and all you have to do is to recognize the right answer when you see it.

DIVERGENT PRODUCTION OF UNITS

Visual Units (DVU)

When we search broadly for items of information of a somewhat general kind, the cue for recall is naturally a class idea, in response to which we give members of the class. This is true of all categories of information, including visual-figural.

Look at the two simple objects in *Figure 6.1*. The problem is to take each figure in turn and to say what more complex, familiar objects could be made of it by adding lines. For drawing *A* you could say: arrow, bird's beak, triangle, wedge, the letter *x*, and so on. What else might be made? For drawing *B* you might say: eye, mouth, ring, tin can, hamburger, hoop, and so on. The objects you give are determined by the shapes of the given lines, hence the things produced are in the visual-figural category, even though they are named. Naming is merely a matter of translation for the sake of communication. It should also be clear that each given figure establishes a class cue to which you respond with class members.

Figure 6.1

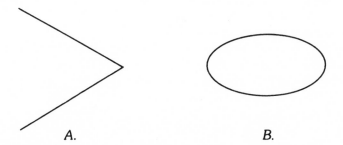

A.   B.

Symbolic Units (DSU)

A common task involving *DSU* calls for producing words in a specified class, such as: words containing the letter *e;* words ending in *tion;* or words rhyming with *grip*. The letter *e* appears most frequently in English words, so the first-mentioned class is very large. We could make the class smaller by specifying that each word should contain two *e*'s. Words rhyming with *grip* include: drip, slip, sip, pip, zip, and so on. From this illustration it is apparent that *DSU* is of special value to poets.

The other examples suggest that *DSU* is of special value in doing crossword puzzles. For each given definition of a word, and a given number of letters (two specifications), you think in turn of possible words that approach satisfaction of those requirements, until the right one comes. With part of the puzzle completed, you have additional specifications that are helpful, since they narrow the class of the word you need.

Semantic Units (DMU)

A task that would exercise ability *DMU* in rather pure form specifies a class in a limited area of meaning. For example, you might be asked to name all the objects you can think of that are both man-made and smaller than a baseball. Your list might contain: watch, diamond ring, key, razor blade, tennis ball, pill, etc. Such a task is found in the test called *Ideational Fluency*, because fluency of thinking is the nature of the task.

It can be said that Thomas A. Edison must have been very high in *DMU* because when an experiment failed he had a number of ideas for new experiments. Sir Winston Churchill, the great British statesman, was also described as a man high with respect to ideational fluency. It was said that in a group discussion, whenever a question or problem came up, Sir Winston always had several ideas to offer.

Another test for *DMU* is called *Plot Titles*. The task is to suggest different names or titles for a short, short story, as if writing headlines for a news story. The following story could be used in such a task:

> *Mr. Ima Glutton entered a fishing contest to see who could catch the largest red snapper. The fish he caught early in the contest looked very small. Thinking that it could not possibly win, he cooked it and ate it. As things turned out, no other fish was caught. Having no fish to show, he lost the $200 prize.*

What names can you give for this story? A name must of course be relevant; it must be reasonable and say something about the story. You might give titles like the following:

> *The man who ate the prize.*
> *The fishing contest.*
> *A small fish for a big prize.*
> *Red snappers were scarce.*
> *The red-snapper contest.*
> *A prize nobody won.*
> *Ima lived up to his name.*

And so on; there is much room for titles. In such a task some people give long lists and some only short lists in the time allowed. Although each answer is not expressed in only one word, the answer produced is a unit, since it is a single idea. The answers do not have to be clever in order to count for a score for *DMU*. We shall see later that clever answers, like the first or the third above, indicate another divergent-production ability.

Behavioral Units (DBU)

For illustrating *DBU* there is a task parallel to the *Ideational Fluency* test for *DMU*. The class specified as a cue and the responses to it must, of course, refer to personal feelings and behavior. The problem is to suggest different things a person might say if he were both *ENVIOUS* and *DISAPPOINTED*. Possible answers are:

> *I just can't seem to beat that fellow.*
> *I wish I could get the kind of grades Betty does.*
> *And I worked so hard. What is his secret?*
> *Why so some people have all the luck?*

In a test for *DBU* the class cue can be provided by means of a bodily expression, as in *Figure 6.2*, for example. What different things could the man with his hands to his head be saying or thinking? It might be:

> *What an awful headache.*
> *What have I done?*
> *I'm awfully sleepy.*
> *Let me think that over.*
> *I lost again.*

What are your own suggestions?

Figure 6.2

Now you might think that in this particular test that each answer represents merely a cognition. Why is divergent production featured? If only one response were considered right and were so keyed, and you gave only one response, it would be a test of *CBU* — cognition of behavioral units. Only a picture that is used because it has a clearly "right" answer would be used in that case. The fact that several responses are all permissible and relevant puts it in the divergent-production category.

DIVERGENT PRODUCTION OF CLASSES

In any of the content areas of information it is often possible to classify the same collection of items in more than one way. Take playing cards, for example. You could classify them by suit — diamonds, clubs, spades, and hearts; by values — numbers and faces: or in two classes — face cards and number cards; or in other ways. Many tasks used as tests take advantage of this possibility, in assessment of divergent production of classes. Some people who face such a task, but very few, classify the items in one way and see no other possible way. Others produce a large number of classes. The people in the latter group are high in one or more of the abilities of special interest here.

Visual Classes (DVC)

In *Chapter 3* (p. 27) you saw sets of four letters each used to illustrate visual-figural classes. Each set had at least one attribute in common. We can also use letters to illustrate the *DVC* activity, as in *Figure 6.3*. From the eight given letters, how many classes of at least three letters each can you make? The following classes are examples:

O C B   (They contain curved lines.)
E T H   (contain horizontal lines)
E N H   (contain parallel lines)
X N H   (open at top and bottom)
X E C   (open at the right)
E N T H (contain vertical lines)

Figure 6.3

X E N O C T H B

Symbolic Classes (DSC)

In applying the multiple-grouping kind of task with symbolic items we may use the first names of people, as in the following list:

1. Alice   4. Carrie   6. Felix
2. Jim   5. Bill   7. Anne
3. Arthur

Some suggested classes are:

1, 3, 7 (begin with A)   2, 5, 7 (of one syllable)
1, 4, 7 (end in E)   1, 5, 6 (contain L)
4, 5, 7 (have double consonant)

Semantic Classes (DMC)

For multiple grouping of words in terms of their meanings, the following list is an example:

1. robin   3. boat   5. wasp   7. alligator
2. airplane   4. whale   6. knife

Some alternative classes are:

1, 2, 5 (fly in the air)   1, 4, 5, 7 (animals)
2, 3, 6 (man-made)   3, 4, 7 (found in water)
5, 6, 7 (dangerous)

A test for *DMC* of a rather different nature is called *Brick Uses*. The instruction is simply: *List all the uses you can for a common brick.* In this test, some people give a list like this: *build a house, build a church, build a walk, build a chimney, build a barbecue pit,* and so on. If the list is long, this performance indicates a high degree of fluency of ideas (ability *DMU*). Other people, however, break out of this rut and give a number of unusual uses like: *use as a doorstop, as bookends, as baseball bases, to filter water,* and *to throw at a yowling cat.* What such a person is doing is going from one *class* of uses to another — divergent production of classes, showing unusual strength in *DMC.* Evidently this person is putting the task at a higher level, using a broader class cue, which extends his range of possible answers. Broadening a class cue may often make possible responses that would otherwise escape.

Because of *DMC's* role in opening up new possibilities for things that we know, it makes some contributions to invention and creative thinking in general. How often do you need to adapt a familiar object to some unusual use? Being able to do so is resourcefulness.

One of the current ecological problems is what to do with the mounting number of worn-out automobile tires. There have been some useful answers to this problem. Used tires have been dumped in the ocean to make homes for fish. They are also ground up and mixed with green latex to produce a kind of artificial turf. It is helpful in dealing with a problem such as this to think of all the attributes of the object (remember the attribute-listing method mentioned in *Chapter 2*) and of places in which the attributes could be of value. Thinking of one attribute after another, of course, means moving from class to class, or *DMC*.

Behavioral Classes (DBC)

One test of *DBC* gives a list of verbal statements to be classified, such as:

1. *Here's your hat; you shouldn't keep her waiting*
2. *Can you prove it*
3. *How boring*
4. *I didn't expect that*
5. *Next time, do as I say*
6. *I wish you had done better*
7. *Can I depend on you*
8. *Leave me alone*

Punctuation marks are intentionally omitted so as not to tie the statements in a more fixed manner; to permit flexibility in their interpretation and use. Possible classes are:

1, 3, 8 *(repelling someone)*
2, 4, 7 *(showing mistrust)*
3, 5, 6 *(showing displeasure)*
4, 5, 6 *(disappointed)*

One place in daily life in which *CBC* has been found relevant is in the performances of probation officers. Their success in dealing with parolees should depend very much upon how well they can sense the attitudes and trends of feeling and thinking of their clients. They must be open-minded and flexible in doing so, leaving room for changes in interpretation. Once they classify a parolee's disposition, or diagnose his behavior, they are ready to apply treatment. The parallel ability *DBC* should also be useful in this connection.

DIVERGENT PRODUCTION OF RELATIONS

A general comment can be made regarding tasks for divergent production of relations in all areas of information. Such tests may call for completion of a *relationship*, either by giving to the examinee two units for which he is to supply a number of different relations, or by giving him a unit and a relation to which he is to respond with other units. A problem of the first type might be: *In what different ways are a father and daughter related?* For the other type we could ask: *What members of a family tree are opposite in sex to a father?* The second type of problem has a larger potential number of answers as a rule and is more commonly used.

Symbolic Relations (DSR)

There are no known good examples of tasks for *DVR*, so we skip that one. For *DSR* there is a *Number Rules* test that asks one to relate numbers in different ways in order to reach a certain goal number. Numbers can be related by means of the fundamental numerical operations. One problem reads: *Start with 2 and arrive at 6.* The different answers could be: *2 × 3; 2 + 4; 2 + 2 + 2; 2 × 2 + 2;* or *2 + 5 − 1.*

Try another problem: *Starting with 3, arrive at 12.* Actually the number of possibilities here is very great.

Success of students in 9th-grade mathematics has been found to depend in part on ability *DSR.*

Semantic Relations (DMR)

You have already seen that where relations are concerned, tasks involving analogies provide good test problems. A multiple-analogies test is in the following form:

> *Supply in the blanks a number of different pairs of things related as the two given objects are related:*
> *ATHLETE is to SCHOLAR as* _____ *is to* _____.
> *ATHLETE is to SCHOLAR as* _____ *is to* _____.
> *ATHLETE is to SCHOLAR as* _____ *is to* _____.
> *ATHLETE is to SCHOLAR as* _____ *is to* _____.

You need to think of different ways in which athlete and scholar are related, and then for each of those ways you are to supply another pair of things related in the same way. You could say: *playing field is to library, brawn is to brain,* or *practice is to study.* What else could be said?

Associational Fluency is of the kind in which you are given one thing and a relation is clearly implied. One problem reads: *List all the things you can think of that mean nearly the same as "wet."* You could say: *moist, watery, soaking, saturated, dripping, soggy,* and so on. The implied relation is similarity. In such a test the relation might be opposite to, part of, or descriptive of, and the like.

DMR has been found related to achievement in a certain English course. This would be natural, if the teacher who assigned the grades put a high value on choice of words. The student who can generate many alternative words in relational connections has a better chance of expressing himself adequately. *DMR* was also found related to grades in history, which may mean that there was an emphasis in the course on producing multiple relations between historical events and personalities.

Behavioral Relations (DBR)

As in the area of cognition, tasks that involve *DMR* can be most readily illustrated where the relations are between two people. Given some sketches of heads of several people, each with a different expression, the examinee is to list as many ways as possible in which they can be related. With only three expressive faces in *Figure 6.4*, it is possible to produce as many as three relations — *CA*, *CB*, and *AB*. *C* is whistling to *A* and she is responding positively; *C* is whistling at *B*, but she is responding negatively. As for *A* and *B*, *A* is telling *B* something that she does not want to hear.

Figure 6.4

Select pairs of these expressive faces in which the two persons have some personal relation with one another. It is possible to relate all possible pairs.

DIVERGENT PRODUCTION OF SYSTEMS

Visual Systems (DVS)

Organizing elements in various ways is the action in divergent production of systems. For *DVS* there is a test that supplies four elementary figures to be organized so as to make border designs, as seen in fabrics or wallpaper. One problem is seen in *Figure 6.5*. What border designs could you make? Scores in such a test have been found predictive of a teacher's rating of her students in designing.

Figure 6.5

Given:

Possible designs:

1.

2.

3.

4.

Another *DVS* test calls for the production of different arrangements of three given letters in monograms: *What different arrangements could be made with the letters J, S, and G?* In still another task, examinees are given elementary figures like those in *Figure 6.5* and are told: *Construct stated familiar objects out of them, such as a face, a flower, or a clown.*

The construction of complex things out of parts is so common in daily life that ability DVS must be useful for all of us. People especially concerned with this kind of activity are designers, architects, and inventors, although it must not be assumed that they always start with parts to make wholes. Sometimes one starts with ideas of wholes and looks for parts. But even then there is an organizational problem, and rearrangements must also often be made.

Symbolic Systems (DSS)

An illustration of a DSS task is found in a certain type of arithmetical problem. One problem reads:

> If you have 2 dollars to spend (all of it), and if a package of chewing gum costs 5 cents, a chocolate bar 10 cents, and a pencil 15 cents, in how many different ways can you spend the 2 dollars? How many packages of gum, how many chocolate bars, and how many pencils would require exactly 2 dollars?

A few possibilities could be:

Chewing gum	Candy bars	Pencils
8	10	4
6	8	6
2	7	8

Semantic Systems (DMS)

Semantic systems should include such complex things as plans for organizations, scientific theories, and plots for novels, but none of these is very manageable for use in psychological tests. Most DMS tests have been in the form of composing sentences. Until it is scientifically demonstrated that the same organizing ability applies to both sentence construction and the more complex system building, we shall just have to assume that this is true.

One sentence-construction task calls for writing sentences of only four words each, with initial letters of the four words given. The following item is an example:

w⎯⎯⎯⎯ f⎯⎯⎯⎯ s⎯⎯⎯⎯ p⎯⎯⎯⎯

Alternative answers might be:

> Who found several pigs?
> Will Francis stop poaching?
> Wallace framed some pictures.
> Willing friars send postcards.

In another successful test for *DMS* each problem presents three words, usually nouns, and asks you to write different sentences each containing all three. The words might be: *army, desert,* and *fish.* The three objects are to be interrelated in various ways.

Behavioral Systems (DBS)

The following illustration of a *DBS* task describes three people, and the examinee is to construct different story plots that involve all three. Suppose the given people are *A, a fearful woman, B, an angry man,* and *C, an unhappy child.* What stories could be organized about them? Some sample stories are:

> *C has broken his father's fishing rod. The father, B, is furious. The mother, A, is fearful of what B will do to C, who feels guilty.*

> *A got home too late to get dinner on time, which angers her husband, B. C is sad to see his mother berated.*

> *A has severely damaged the family car, which infuriates her husband, B. C feels sorry for his mother in the family quarrel.*

DIVERGENT PRODUCTION OF TRANSFORMATIONS

Making alternative changes provides another category of divergent-production abilities. Such abilities have two reasons for contributing to creative thinking, for they offer both fluency and flexibility in thinking.

Visual Transformations (DVT)

There is a rich supply of tasks known to involve *DVT*, from which we may draw illustrations. Every time you are making over what you see, you are engaging in *DVT*. In *Figure 6.6* are four sets of squares whose sides are composed of matches so they can be easily removed. One problem is: *Remove any matches you wish so as to leave three squares, with no extra matches left over.* You are to do it differently in each set.

Figure 6.6

There are 15 different solutions to this problem. How many can you produce?

DVT is often involved in puzzles. Tell a friend that half of eight is three and that you can prove it. The proof is to write the figure 8 in nice round upper and lower parts (8) then draw a vertical line down the center (ʘ). The right half is a (3). Tell another friend, who is uninitiated by having had the other problem, that you can prove that half of eight is zero. In this case the proof is to draw a horizontal line through the 8 after which each half makes a zero. Tell still another person you can prove half of 12 is 7. You have to make the 12 in a Roman numeral (XII) and then draw a horizontal line across the middle (X̶I̶I̶). The upper part is VII, or 7.

Symbolic Transformations (DST)

Symbolic transformations can occur when certain words are hidden inside other words. In the test *Hidden Word Production,* you are told to hide a word such as "former." This might be done in any of the following ways:

> *formerly one dollar*
> *yourself or Mervin*
> *sea stuff or mermaid*
> *arrest all informers*
> *uniform erasers*

There is no evidence as yet concerning the relation of *DST* to performance in mathematics, but a relationship would seem reasonably expected. In fact, the roles of all of the symbolic abilities seem to be so apparent in mathematics that one could infer that the brain operates according to mathematical principles or mathematical logic. The fact that there are clearly parallel abilities dealing with the other kinds of informational content suggests that the brain does the best it can in applying the same logic in those other areas. The symbolic information in mathematics is always precisely defined, hence the value of applying mathematical thinking wherever we can and wherever it is important to do so.

Semantic Transformations (DMT)

Recall for a moment the story that illustrated a task for *DMU* — the man who ate the fish he caught and thereby lost the prize. If we count only the *clever* answers to such a story we obtain a score for *DMT*. Of the sample responses given there, at least two can be regarded as clever — *"The man who ate the prize"* and *"A small fish for a big prize."* A clever title is likely to be amusing because transformations are more generally amusing, as was mentioned in connection with ability *CMT*, in *Chapter 4*. A man eating a prize is quite a shift from what would ordinarily be expected. In the other title, the shift is from a prize awarded for a big fish to a prize awarded for a little fish.

From these interpretations we see that transformations are involved. Another title that might be regarded as clever for the same story is *"Were red snappers on strike?"* Implicit are two transformations. One is in giving fish human characteristics; men strike on their jobs, fish do not. In the word "strike" we also have a pun. Still another clever title would be *"A $200 fish dinner,"* a little high-priced even nowadays.

Divergent transformations provide a very important source of originality in daily life, for they produce novel results. This is true in all content areas, but since most problems in daily life are in the semantic area, it is there that the statement is most significant. Suggestions on how to improve skills in these performances will be given in *Chapter 10*.

Behavioral Transformations (DBI)

In a task representing *DBI* the examinee is given a short story plot, with the instruction to revise the story in several different ways. One story reads as follows:

> *Two sisters, A and B, are romantically interested in the same young man, C. One day he comes to their home unexpectedly. They both greet him warmly and he takes them both to a movie. What else could have happened?*

Here are a few possibilities:

> *A sees him coming and hides B's best dress, which she wanted to wear. C finds out about it and thereafter dates only B.*
>
> *B tells C that her sister A thinks C is a liar. C has a talk with A and learns that B was not telling the truth.*
>
> *A and B both flatter C until he is not sure which he likes better and in the future avoids them both.*

What else could have happened? Every revision is a transformation of a behavioral system.

DIVERGENT PRODUCTION OF IMPLICATIONS

Remember that an implication is one thing expected from another, one thing suggesting another, or one thing extended in some manner.

In divergent production of implications, we go to a number of different things from one given item of information.

Visual Implications (DVI)

A very natural task for *DVI* presents common objects in outline form, such as household furniture or articles of clothing, and you are asked to add to them some decorative embellishments. The more different decorative ideas you offer, the higher your score. In this *Decorations* test, the same object is presented twice, giving more room for different alternative implications.

The designer of clothing and artists of different kinds keep adding details to produce more finished appearances. The things added are implied by shapes and colors already there. Such embellishment can be overdone; the artist's judgment should tell him when to stop. But some possibly stop short of completion because of a lack of ideas, or because of their deficiency in ability *DVT*.

Symbolic Implications (DSI)

A natural place to look for examples of *DSI* tasks would be in mathematics. One problem that demonstrates *DSI* in particular presents two simple equations such as:

$$B - C = D \text{ and } A + D = Z$$

What other equations can be deduced from these two? A few are:

$$Z - A = D$$
$$C + D = B$$
$$A + B - C = Z$$
$$B - Z = C - A$$

The value of being able to generate a number of different equations from one that is given is obvious.

Semantic Implications (DMI)

A test called *Possible Jobs* presents a pictorial symbol in the form of a familiar object, and you are to suggest alternative kinds of jobs or occupations that it could stand for. Look at the symbol in *Figure 6.7*, for example, a flower. What occupations does a flower suggest? It might represent a florist, of course, but it could also stand for a gardener, a horticulturist, a seed merchant, a botanist, and so on. Although the object is given in pictorial form, it is a real object, hence is semantic and the answers are semantic.

Figure 6.7

A different kind of task for *DMI* calls for planning elaboration. The given problem provides the outline of a plan for accomplishing a certain goal, such as putting on an amateur play for paid admissions. Such a plan needs numerous details in the way of actions and materials in order to make the plan work. Supplying a list of such details is a matter of *DMI*, the details being implied by the outline.

Behavioral Implications (DBI)

It is well established that the act of seeing problems involves seeing implications. Where one problem is seen it is a matter of cognition of an implication. Where a number of alternative implications must be generated it is a matter of divergent production. For a task for *DBI* the problem question might be:

> *What personal problems can a brother and sister have with each other?*

A list of problems in answer to this question might be:

> *Sister dislikes brother's friends.*
> *Sister tries to dominate younger brother.*
> *They can't agree on whom to invite to a party.*
> *Sister makes fun of brother's clothes.*
> *Both want to use the family car, etc.*

RELATION OF DIVERGENT PRODUCTION TO COGNITION

In the chapter on memory abilities it was pointed out that if there has been no cognition there will be no memory. We can now add that if there has been no memory there is no divergent production, for the latter depends upon retrieval from the memory store. A simple deduction is that if there is no previous cognition there is no divergent production. In turn, this suggests that we can never have an idea that is 100 percent new.

Although ordinary IQ scales involve primarily tests of cognition and almost none of divergent production, we can still expect some degree of relationship between the two kinds of abilities. The reason for the *lack* of relationship is that what we cognize is not necessarily remembered and what we remember is not always easily retrieved. But the kinds of dependency just mentioned suggest that at least some relation does exist. It does, but the correlation is low and it is a one-way relation.

When scores from divergent-production tests are studied in relation to IQs of the same individuals, we find an interesting kind of relationship. Individuals of low IQ have only low scores in divergent-production tests. This statement should be qualified, for this fact has been well-established only when both IQ and divergent-production tests are primarily geared for semantic abilities. When IQs are high, however, divergent production can be low as well as high in the same individuals. We may sum up this situation by saying that verbal IQ puts an upper limit on semantic divergent-production performance, and that high IQ does not ensure high divergent-production ability. Because of the importance of divergent-production for creative thinking, we can expect similar relations of creative performance to IQ. Thus, we may make the further deduction that there are many creative underachievers but very few overachievers in relation to IQ. Again, this may be limited to the semantic area.

SUMMARY

Divergent-production abilities are concerned with a broad kind of search for information to be retrieved from the memory store to meet given situations. A situation commonly presents some class idea that serves as a cue for retrieval of items of information, which may be within any of the product categories, in any content area. Quite a number of divergent-production abilities have been demonstrated by factor analysis and were illustrated by means of representative tests in this chapter.

The greatest importance of divergent-production abilities is in connection with creative thinking, where many alternative ideas need to be brought to light with ease. Since creative thinking is an important aspect of problem solving, these abilities are also important in that connection.

It has been found that a high IQ is a necessary condition for having at least high semantic divergent-production abilities, but it is by no means a sufficient condition. We should therefore not expect all high-IQ individuals to be highly creative. A large proportion of them are not.

CHAPTER SEVEN

Focused Search: Convergent Production

Convergent production is the other kind of productive thinking. It also is concerned with retrieval of items of information from memory storage for use in answering questions and solving problems. Whereas in divergent production a number of alternative answers are wanted and will do, in convergent production only one answer will ordinarily satisfy the requirements of the question or problem. Only one answer is considered correct.

But do not let this last statement become your definition of convergent production, for in all other operation categories except divergent production there is only "one right answer" also, as in tests for abilities in those areas. Do not forget the "production" part of the name of the operation that this chapter is about.

The convergent answer that you give may be the one that you have already learned in connection with the given information. If you are asked, "What do we call the wife of a king?" you say "queen," for that is the connection that you have learned. On the other hand, sometimes your answer must bridge a gap; it was not previously learned in connection with the given information. If you are told that Tom is taller than Dick and that Dick is taller than Harry, you can conclude that Tom is also taller than Harry without being told so specifically. Convergent production is the area of logic-tight deductions. That which is called deductive thinking belongs in this category.

It is true that we may engage in much divergent production en route to the right answer in a convergent-production task — convergent, that is, so far as the goal is concerned. We have not finished until we come to the right answer. We weigh or evaluate each divergently produced item, and we accept or reject it. Evaluations are not always correct, so we sometimes leave an incorrect answer to stand for a solution to a convergent-production problem.

CONVERGENT PRODUCTION OF UNITS

Our present knowledge concerning kinds of tasks that should represent the convergent production of units is somewhat limited, but it is possible to make some good guesses where knowledge is lacking. The guessing can be based in part upon the nature of representative tests for parallel abilities in the *Structure of Intellect*.

Visual Units (NVU)[1]

A kind of task that should illustrate *NVU* is commonly known as a "following-directions" test. The instruction for each item tells what to draw or to write. What is produced might be in any of the content areas. For *NVU* it would naturally be visual figures; simple ones for units and complex ones for systems. The following items could comprise a *NVU* test:

1. *Make the letter T upside down.*
2. *Make the letter O wider than it is tall.*
3. *Draw just the outline of a bird in flight.*
4. *Make a half-inch square with an X within it that is as large as possible.*

Symbolic Units (NSU)

The following items should serve in a test for *NSU:*

1. *What letter comes before R in the alphabet?*
2. *What letter follows Q in English words?*
3. *What is the smallest prime number?*
4. *What is the largest perfect square less than 100?*

In daily life, one problem that may well involve this ability is encountered in the writing of newspaper headlines, which must use available space properly. This task is also somewhat divergent in that alternative headlines might do as well. In doing crossword puzzles, the requirement of fitting spaces with a word of a certain meaning and ending in *E* should point to a particular word.

Semantic Units (NMU)

For *NMU* a number of good illustrations could be cited. Some of the *NMU* tasks involve naming, where the name, of course, stands for a

---

[1]*N* is the symbol for convergent production because its initial letter *C* has been applied to cognition.

meaningful concept, like a class idea. In some *NMU* tasks it is *related* things that must be named. In one test an object is given and you are *to respond with the smallest whole of which the given object is a part.* Here are a few items:

    1. leaf   2. cent   3. sister   4. Tuesday   5. word

The specification, *smallest whole of which the given object is a part,* should leave no room for doubt, with rare exceptions. The answers are: *twig, nickel, family, week,* and *phrase.*

Another *NMU* test gives enough of the attributes of an object so that only one thing could be the answer. In the following items, give the name of the object that applies to each set of specifications:

1. *partially white bird, found near the ocean, revered by Mormons*
2. *warm, living, red fluid*
3. *orange-colored root vegetable*
4. *mirth producer at a circus*
5. *afternoon theater program*

It may be noted that these items read like definitions. Each one names as many attributes (class features) as are necessary to point directly at one thing and no other. This should remind you of the discussion of meaning in *Chapter 2,* where it was pointed out that a typical semantic unit has an aura or context of class ideas. In case you have not produced the semantic units called for by the items, they are (in order): *seagull, blood, carrot, clown,* and *matinee.*

CONVERGENT PRODUCTION OF CLASSES

As yet there are no tasks known to represent convergent production of behavioral information, so we proceed to the next product category — classes. Such abilities have not been investigated. Theoretically there should be abilities of this kind and they should be important especially in connection with legal matters and perhaps in the field of ethics, insofar as there are established principles of conduct.

Visual Classes (NVC)

A natural type of convergent-production task would present a collection of units of the same content category, which are to be sorted into a few mutually exclusive classes. An example of such a test is shown in *Figure 7.1.* In a partitioning exercise, the nine figures shown are to be sorted into a small number of classes. This task resembles some that were used to illustrate the divergent production of classes in the preceding chapter. The difference is that here no figure is put in more than one class; the classes are mutually exclusive. The three classes may be described as follows: *3, 4, 8 (contain curved lines); 2, 6, 7 (triangles);* and *1, 5, 8, 9 (four-sided figures).*

Figure 7.1

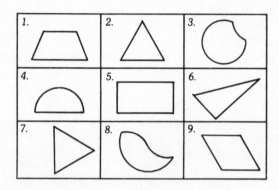

Symbolic Classes (NSC)

For an *NSC* task, let us take a second type of convergent-production test, known as an "exclusion test." In the following items, each containing four nonsense words of four letters each, which word does not belong in the class with the rest?

1. *A A B C*	*A C A D*	*A F G H*	*A C Q A*
2. *X U V W*	*A B C D*	*M N O P*	*E F G H*
3. *B C D D*	*E F G H*	*J K L L*	*P Q R R*
4. *A B B B*	*E F F F*	*I J J J*	*P O O O*
5. *K A B C*	*K H I J*	*L O P Q*	*K U V W*

The answers, with reasons, are:

1. *A F G H*   (*Each of other words contains two A's.*)
2. *X U V W*   (*Others have all letters in alphabetical order.*)
3. *E F G H*   (*Others end in double letters.*)
4. *P O O O*   (*The single letter precedes the repeated one in the alphabet.*)
5. *L O P Q*   (*All others begin with K.*)

In this test, as in others of the same type, some cognitive ability, in this case *CSC*, is also involved, because the examinee must cognize what the class feature is, and this aspect of the task is not always easy. It is an *NVC* task as well, because in performing it one is actually sorting a set of items into two classes, despite the fact that one class has only one member.

Semantic Classes (NMC)

A partitioning task that illustrates *NMC* uses the following list of meaningful words that are to be sorted in classes of two to four words each:

1. blue	4. heavy	7. little	10. orange
2. knife	5. large	8. long	11. red
3. putter	6. light	9. pliers	12. miniature

The classes and reasons for them are:

$$1, 10, 11 \ldots \ldots \ldots (colors)$$
$$2, 3, 9 \ldots \ldots \ldots (tools)$$
$$4, 6 \ldots \ldots \ldots \ldots (pertain\ to\ weight)$$
$$5, 7, 8, 12 \ldots (pertain\ to\ size)$$

It has been demonstrated that ability *NMC* is related to the learning of concepts, where the concept is a principle or class idea. The parallel cognition ability, *CMC*, is also generally an asset in learning a concept, but whereas *NMC* is helpful almost from the beginning of the learning experience, with increasing value, *CMC* may actually be a handicap at first. This may mean that if a person is too ready to see classes where none exist, he makes errors of classification. The value of *CMC* does increase after some initial experiences with the items of information.

CONVERGENT PRODUCTION OF RELATIONS

Visual Relations (NVR)

For illustrating tasks for the corresponding cognition abilities, analogy tests have been very useful. With modifications the same kind of tasks are also suitable for convergent-production abilities. For testing cognition abilities the analogy tests have been in multiple-choice form, with alternative answers given, one of which is correct. For convergent production the test must be in completion form; the answer must be produced.

The items in *Figure 7.2* are from a figure-analogies-completion test. The figure must be drawn to complete the second relationship. For item

Figure 7.2

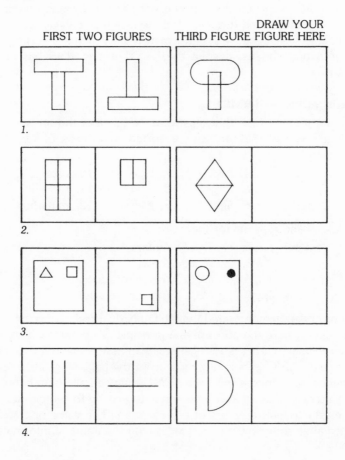

1, the same figure should be drawn as that which appears in the third square, only in an inverted position. For item 2, a single triangle should be drawn, like the upper half of the figure in the third square. For item 3, a dot in the lower-right corner of the fourth square is called for. Two relations are involved in this item. The object at the left is omitted and the object at the right is moved down. In item 4, the two objects are moved together to form one figure. Doing that to the objects in the third square should leave the letter *D*. Incidentally, the last two items get dangerously close to involving transformations, as well as, or even instead of, relations. It depends upon how you structure the given information.

The items just considered also involve the ability *CVR* to some extent because you must see what the relation is between the first two figures. We could probably reduce the importance of *CVR* in this test by telling the examinee what the relation is. We could go even further by giving a following-directions test. For example, we could say: *Draw a mirror image;* or *Invert the figure;* or *Draw just the upper half.* All these directions involve relations.

Symbolic Relations (NSR)

An analogies-completion test also exists for *NSR*. The relation between the first two units is made easier to see by presenting an additional sample relationship, as in the following:

1. *thumb*	*hum*	*want*	*an*	*maiden*	?
2. *sell*	*tell*	*louse*	*mouse*	*ear*	?
3. *went*	*wont*	*pant*	*pint*	*stint*	?
4. *pistol*	*piston*	*par*	*pat*	*sine*	?

The right answers and reasons follow:
1. *aide (from all but end letters of preceding word)*
2. *far (initial letter next in the alphabet)*
3. *stunt (vowel is second in alphabetical order)*
4. *sing (last letter is second following in the alphabet)*

Ability *NSR* is known to be of some use in achievement in 9th-grade algebra. In algebra, of course, relations between numbers or letters are found everywhere, and the student must give convergent answers. In fact, one should expect most of the convergent-production abilities concerned with symbolic information to be involved in mathematical operations.

Semantic Relations (NMR)

In discussion of *NMU* tasks, one of the tests mentioned is also in part concerned with *NMR*. The relation involved is part-whole — the examinee names the smallest whole of which the given object is a part. The given objects in the test included: *leaf, cent, sister, Tuesday,* and *word.*

There is a special kind of association test that involves *NMR* in another way. The following items are typical. What word is related to both given words in each pair?

1. *nonsense* _____ *bed*
2. *recline* _____ *deceive*

3. hit	_____	*fruit drink*
4. tiresome	_____	*drilling*
5. sphere	_____	*dance*

You may have had to reach far out to find some of the answers. For these five items the related words are: *bunk, lie, punch, boring,* and *ball.* The task could be made perhaps even more convergent by asking for a word related to three given words, such as *"cottage, mouse, sandwich,"* to which the answer is *"cheese."*

NMR has been found related to achievement in a course in history. This probably means that the teacher, textbook, or the examinations emphasized drawing conclusions regarding relations among events or among historical persons, or between persons and events. This, of course, goes beyond teaching isolated facts, which is good educational policy.

CONVERGENT PRODUCTION OF SYSTEMS

Visual Systems (NVS)

No tasks have been designed for *NVS,* as yet. It can be suggested, however, that a following-directions form of task could be applied in this connection. The thing to be produced need only be complex, as compared with those in tasks for *NVU.* Perhaps the following problems would do:

> Draw three circles touching one another, one above and two below.
>
> Draw two squares, one above the other. Put diagonal lines in each square. Connect with a straight line the points at which the diagonal lines cross.

As elsewhere, it takes at least three units to make a system, and that condition we have in both these items.

An old problem that must surely involve *NVS* is given in the form of a diagram in *Figure 7.3:*

> The diagram is a map of an old man's farm. The circles represent fruit trees. The father has four sons, to whom he wants to leave his farm, divided in equal parts in the same shape, and each with the same number of fruit trees. How should the farm be divided? The division should be along the lines given within the farm. You would make the division lines heavier.

Figure 7.3

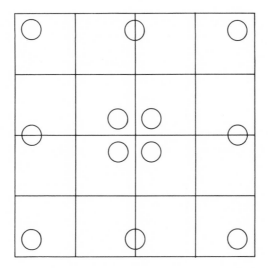

You will find the solution in *Figure 7.4*. There is no doubt about the systematic nature of the solution, and it is a convergent problem.

Symbolic Systems (NSS)

The illustrative tasks for *NSS* that are given here are concerned with systems in the form of sequences. There are, of course, other kinds of symbolic systems. The first task is a kind of problem that you may have seen in some magazine: *Start with one given word, and, by changing only one letter at a time, keep changing words until you arrive at another given word.* For example, suppose the starting word is *SET*. By changing one letter at a time, arrive at the word *CRY*. If you would like to try to solve this problem, do so now because the sequence is given in the next sentence. The solution should be: *SET, SAT, SAY, DAY, DRY,* and finally *CRY*.

In the second illustrative problem, you are to start with one given number and to arrive at another, doing some numerical operations in between. If the starting number is 6 and the end number is *18*, in what order should these three operations (+3, ÷2, and ×3) be applied? The order should be: ÷2, +3, and ×3.

The second task, particularly, suggests the probable usefulness of this ability in mathematics, and, indeed, a relation to achievement in 9th-grade algebra has been found. The ability has also been found related to

Figure 7.4

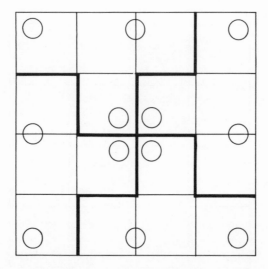

programming for solving problems with computers. In other words, it is one of the indicators of aptitude for computer programming. The computer programmer must lay out a particular sequence of steps for the computer to go through in solving each type of problem.

Semantic Systems (NMS)

Ordering tests are also used for *NMS*. One task asks for the correct ordering of events that are given in random order. The following items are of that nature:

    1. a. *She read the recipe for the second time.*
       b. *She went to the market.*
       c. *She tested to see if the cake was done.*
       d. *She beat the eggs.*
    2. a. *He answered the curtain call.*
       b. *He dressed in his costume for the first act.*
       c. *He put on his makeup.*
       d. *The audience saw the curtain rise for the opening scene.*
    3. a. *The audience filed out of the stadium.*
       b. *A sudden rainstorm caused cancellation of the game.*
       c. *People asked for the return of their money for*

  the game.
  d. The game had reached the second inning.

If you have already decided on the correct orders of events within each problem, compare your orders with the following: *1. b, a, d, c; 2. c, b, d, a;* and *3. d, b, a, c.*

The same kind of task in pictorial form uses cartoon strips. The examinee is asked to unscramble the panels which are presented out of order. If the order depends in part upon behavioral aspects of the events, then ability *NBS* should also be involved. It can be suggested that a detective needs to apply both *NMS* and *NBS* in reconstructing events in a crime.

CONVERGENT PRODUCTION OF TRANSFORMATIONS

  As in the area of divergent production of transformations, we come to abilities that are especially relevant in creative thinking because of the flexibility that they offer despite the fact that there must be "one right answer." The tasks in this area require transformations to meet narrowly prescribed requirements. High-ranking scientists tend to agree that these abilities are the most important for them in their work. They are looking for convergent answers, yet they must be flexible.

Visual Transformations (NVT)

  You have surely seen the popular kind of puzzle that calls for finding human faces hidden in a complex background. The transformations come as you take lines and shapes belonging at first to the general background scene and put them into new objects — faces.

  In a more stylized task known as *Hidden Figures,* you are asked to say which of five simple figures is concealed within each of quite a number of more complex figures. In *Figure 7.5* the five simple figures are shown along with three sample test items: *Which simple figure is concealed in each of them? In item 1, you can find figure D; in item 2, figure A; and in item 3, figure B.* Again, you have to change the functions of certain lines; they are torn out of the more complex figures, so to speak, to make them serve as lines in the simple figures. Your brain reorganizes the arrangements of lines.

  In presenting tasks for the parallel ability *DVT* in the preceding chapter, a match-problem test was used. In a set of squares formed of match sticks you were told to remove any number of match sticks you wished, leaving three squares. This result could be reached in a number of different ways, so the problem was divergent. In *Figure 7.6,* for a

Figure 7.5

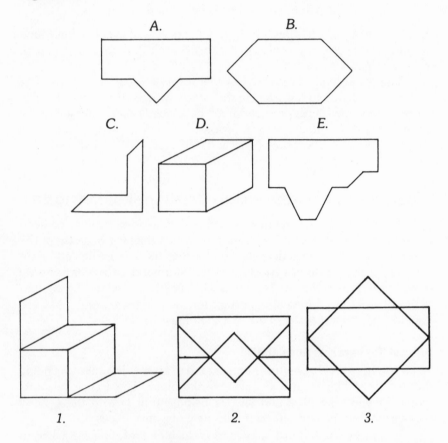

convergent task, try to remove six sticks leaving exactly two squares. It takes quite a jump in your thinking to solve this problem. As long as you think in terms of leaving two small squares, you fail. The statement of the problem says nothing about the size of the squares to be left. One remaining square has to be four times the size of the other, which is a reinterpretation of the problem — a transformation. If you still lack the solution, just remove the two sticks at the upper left and all four of the sticks within the large square at the right. You could, of course, remove the two lower-left sticks, or you could leave the large square on the left, but all these solutions are the same in principle, and the task is still convergent.

We should expect ability *NVT* to be useful whenever we do not see things as they really are and we need to produce a revised impression in order to deal with the situation realistically. Low status in *NVT* means a kind of rigidity (there are other kinds). Some people cling to what they think is "reality" to the extent that they do not see things as they really should.

Special groups who need a good amount of working *NVT* are inventors, engineers, and architects. This need does not apply so much to artists, for they rarely encounter hard and fast requirements for what they do. The engineer's bridge must stand up under heavy loads that can be specified, but the artist has freedom of choice. He has only himself and his public to satisfy. For him ability *DVT* is much more important.

Symbolic Transformations (NST)

As mentioned earlier, we encounter transformations of symbolic items of information in camouflaged words. That is, we find words buried in other words. The test *Camouflaged Words* is based upon this principle, and it was designed for *NST*. Each of the following sentences has concealed in it the name of a sport or game. Can you locate it?

1. *Cowardice is not a soldierly attribute.*
2. *To best the Hun, tin goes a long way.*
3. *The white flour in one bin got mixed with the whole-wheat flour in the other.*
4. *One could tell that he was a Mongol from his costume.*
5. *We traced the shipment and found the missing box in Gulfport.*

In case you have not seen the concealed words, they are: *dice, hunting, bingo, golf,* and *boxing,* respectively. You may recall that in an

Figure 7.6

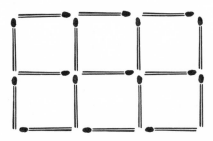

illustrative test for the parallel ability *DST* you have to make up different phrases within which a given word is concealed. That kind of exercise would be the task of the test writer who makes up items for *Camouflaged Words*. Test writing is a creative art.

Semantic Transformations (NMT)

Transformation of a meaning involves a redefinition of something. One case of redefinition is in terms of uses of objects. Several tests have been based upon this kind of shift. One of them presents on the test page a photograph or sketch of a room — kitchen, dining room, living room, or bedroom — with a variety of objects in it. Below the picture is a list of uses or needs, and you are to choose the object from the room that could reasonably fulfill the purpose. You might be asked what could be used to make a fishing rod or a kite. The answer for the fishing rod would be a curtain rod, and for the kite a small light picture frame and a piece of window curtain.

These response objects all involve unusual uses, and they may remind you of tests recommended in the preceding chapter for *DMC* (divergent production of semantic classes). The difference is that for *DMC* the object is given and you are to name the uses, whereas for *NMT* you are given the use to name the object, and only one object would clearly apply.

The emphasis upon adapting objects to meet specified needs or uses suggests that a person's resourcefulness in general depends very much on ability *NMT,* especially where most efficient or successful adaptations are concerned. Problems are frequently encountered in which the customary object is not available and we must adapt something else for the purpose. For example, you are in a small airplane that is downed in some remote, mountainous region. You are in need of shelter from the cold. What can you use? You have wounds and no first-aid kit. How can you take care of them? Some people survive such circumstances by adapting what is available, while other perish. Some of the latter people may have objects available that they could use, but being low in *NMT* they keep those objects within fixed definitions; they cannot redefine.

CONVERGENT PRODUCTION OF IMPLICATIONS

In the convergent-production area we find examples of that ancient operation known as "deduction." In this area, an implication obeys the rules of logical necessity. The synonym "conclusion" applies nicely, if we modify it by adding "correct," to say "correct conclusion." When

Sherlock Holmes got to work on a case his information seemed to lead unerringly to the right conclusion. He had apparently skillfully developed his semantic-implication and behavioral-implication abilities for convergent production — *NMI* and *NBI*.

Visual Implications (NVI)

In the visual area, it is more natural to speak of extensions, foresight, or extrapolation than to speak of conclusions. This kind of implication applies to the problem illustrated in *Figure 7.7*. There you see two items from an Air Force test for pilots. They pertain to the performance in skywriting of letters. Each problem shows two letters to be written by trailing smoke or water vapor in the sky, where the airplane starts its exercise, and where it finishes. In the first problem (for which the solution is shown), by means of dotted lines and arrows indicating directions at certain points, you will see the kinds of turns the plane can make; it cannot turn sharp corners.

The major problem is to complete the two letters of a problem just as efficiently as possible, making the fewest turns and, over all, in traveling the shortest route. The convergent solution is the most efficient one.

The best solution for the unsolved problem on the bottom of *Figure 7.7* would be (1) to fly down the vertical line of the *D;* (2) to make a loop and start over and up the curved part of the *D;* (3) to turn a 180 degree angle as sharply as one can; (4) to turn in order to fly down the vertical line of the *K;* (6) turn right and, on a broad turn, to start down the upper slanting line; and (7) continue to the finish point. All of these maneuvers, one following another, are implied by the starting and finishing positions and the pattern of lines to be traced.

Analogous tasks in daily life can be found in athletics and in industry. Wherever a sequence of movements must be made to accomplish a patterned task, with specifications as to starting and stopping points, and other requirements, there are *NVI* problems. One also thinks of military maneuvers in this connection. This does not rule out the need for divergent production when the specifications and other known conditions are not so very well defined, or when the convergent solution is not obvious.

Symbolic Implications (NSI)

You have seen before in this book the statement that ordinary numerical operations are examples of implications. When you see the information "6 + 2," you convergently produce the implied number "8."

Figure 7.7

The first drawing shows the most economical path that the airplane should take in order to skywrite the letters *V* and *L*. What is the most economical path needed to write the letters *D* and *K* in the second diagram, taking into account the starting and finishing positions shown for the airplane? (Adapted from a U. S. Air Force experimental psychological test.)

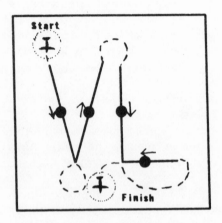

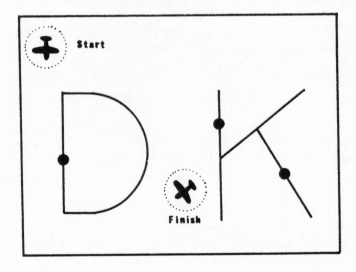

Factor analysis of numerical-operations tests, however, show that they also represent the memory ability *MSI* (parallel to *NSI*) and quite comparably. This reflects the fact that some individuals have put their number-operations implications into memory storage more thoroughly and more functionally than others.

With certain modifications in numerical-operations tasks we can slant them more toward *NSI* and less toward *MSI*. Better yet, we can use operations with letters as in the test to be described next. At the heading of each page are given a set of implications in each of which a given pair of letters implies another single letter, as in the following equations:

$$AB = BA = D \quad BC = CB = F \quad BE = EB = H \quad DE = ED = C$$
$$AD = DA = E \quad BD = DB = A \quad CD = DC = G \quad DF = FD = B$$

These equations are followed by problems that require their use. In each problem, three letters are given, for example, *F, D, C*. Your task is first to substitute for the first two letters their one-letter equivalent. From the given equations, *FD = B*. The second step is to combine this single letter, *B*, with the third letter, *C*, giving *BC*. Finally, we know that *BC = F*, which is the solution. Here are a few more problems to solve:

   1. *A, D, B*   2. *D, E, B*   3. *A, B, E*   4. *D, F, D*

The keyed answers are: *H, F, C,* and *A*, respectively.

NSI is one of the contributors to success in 9th-grade algebra. Its relevance to higher mathematics courses has not been determined, but it clearly seems relevant.

Semantic Implications (NMI)

Ability *NMI* means drawing compulsive, meaningful conclusions. This suggests the traditional subject of logic and syllogisms. A syllogism makes two statements of fact (premises), from which a third fact can be derived logically, with full confidence that it is a valid fact. Syllogisms have been used in a test for *NMI*, with problems like the following:

   1. *All living things breathe.*
      All insects are living things.
      Therefore, _____ .

   2. *No children are voters.*
      Some voters are easily fooled.
      Therefore, _____ .

   3. *Some politicians are honest.*
      All politicians are men.
      Therefore, _____ .

To be correct, any conclusion must take into account both premises. It must also take into account such qualifying words as *"all,"* *"some,"* and *"no."* If you have tried to do these problems, compare your conclusions with the following for items 1 through 3: *all insects breathe; some who are not children are easily fooled;* and *some men are honest.*

We need not confine ourselves to syllogisms to illustrate *NMI*. We may use a "missing-links" task, illustrated by the following three items:

1. *work* _____ _____ _____ *orange*
2. *red* _____ _____ _____ *beer*
3. *thirst* _____ _____ _____ *hole*

The task is to fill the blanks with words in such a way that one word implies the next. There may possibly be other solutions to these problems, but the following sets of words are expected:

1. *job, money, food*
2. *sunset, weather, cold*
3. *drink, water, well*

As you select the words in an item of this test, you have to keep in mind both terminal words. They tend to force one toward convergent answers. In a similar task you would be given a set of four words that are in random order. The problem is to unscramble the order so that each word clearly implies the next.

Still other types of tasks could be cited for *NMI*. The variety of *NMI* tests should be an indication that *NMI* is a widely useful talent. Wherever a person must come to compelling conclusions, with meaningful information, *NMI* is relevant. People who deal with crime and the law come to mind first. The political campaigner who hopes to convince people that his views are sound and the scientist who likes to find facts that force him and others to an incontestable conclusion are also in this group. Planning a chain of arguments, however, also represents *NMS*, the convergent production of semantic systems.

SUMMARY

Convergent production is like divergent production in its dependence upon retrieval of information from memory storage. However, it differs in that the search for information in the memory store is focused by the given information toward a particular answer. Where divergent production is a generation of logical alternatives (logical because they are relevant), convergent production is the generation of logical imperatives. One might say that the results of the former are sufficient, whereas the results of the latter are necessary.

The focusing in retrieval can be on any kind of product, in any content area of information, which means a large number of different abilities or mental functions. In each case, one must come up with the right product, which must satisfy certain specifications or requirements. Sometimes the retrieved product had been stored in just that manner, in connection with cues provided by the problem or question at hand, but sometimes elements are retrieved from which the product is constructed. The former is a case of reconstruction; the latter a case of new construction.

The convergent production of semantic units is of special interest because it often involves giving names for items of information. In the production of classes, in all content areas, the result is a grouping of sets of items into mutually exclusive categories or classes. The production of relations means reasoning by analogy. The production of systems results in orders or other arrangements to serve some prescribed purpose. Producing transformations introduces flexibility into otherwise routine thinking, thus contributing to creative problem solving. Convergently produced implications are our old friends — deductions.

The areas of life that stand to gain most from convergent-production abilities are mathematics, science, and legal matters, including criminology and jurisprudence. In those fields some of the most rigorous thinking exercises are required.

CHAPTER EIGHT

Comparing and Judging Information: Evaluation

You probably do not realize it, but in just about any act that you perform you check, and perhaps double check, what you do. Your nervous system is built to perform in that manner. This is true of both your bodily movements and your mental activities. As you stand erect, for example, balanced on your two feet, any sufficient deviation from maintaining that balance is detected and corrective action occurs. You would notice this process more clearly if you stood on one foot.

To take another example, you reach out to pick up a dime lying on the table. Your hand moves like a guided missile. The dime is the target, and any detected deviation in the path that your hand is taking toward its goal calls for corrective movement. This self-correcting feature of our nervous systems was called most clearly to our attention by those who studied the principles of guided missiles in the field called *cybernetics*. Human information processing in the realm of intelligence also operates according to certain cybernetic principles.

In the processes just described there are two steps. First, there is detection of a deviation from the aim toward the target, and second, there is corrective action. Detection of deviations involves *feedback information* which comes from the action in progress. There is comparison of feedback information concerning what we have done with information about the action needed to hit the target. The latter is *goal information*. If feedback information and goal information match, we need do nothing by way of correction.

The intellectual operation of evaluation is also concerned with a matching of feedback information with goal information, and decision or judgment as to whether or not there is a match, or as to how good the match is. Evaluation applies to information that we have cognized or that we have retrieved from memory storage in productive thinking. If we judge a certain cognized item to be in error or if we have doubts regarding it, we take a second look at our corrective action. If we reject a certain retrieved item that does not satisfy us, we try to retrieve another item or we transform the one we have.

What kinds of comparisons are made, and what are our criteria for judgment? In some cases we know exactly the kind of item we want, and we may have a sample of it available to serve as a model. For example, the question may be, "Is this word spelled exactly like that one?" a question that a proofreader is likely to ask. A worker in a factory may have to decide whether the next article coming off the assembly line is exactly like the model he has before him or that he remembers. In both cases the criterion for judgment is *identity*.

When a model for comparison is not available, one could still have some information regarding the specifications of the item wanted. Suppose we faced the common problem of prying a lid off a tin can, no suitable tool being immediately available. We do know the specifications that such a tool must have. It must be a rigid object that will not break when used for prying against stiff resistance. It must be long enough to provide leverage. It must be light enough to hold in the hand, and have a thin edge that will go under the flange of the lid. We reject using a fingernail (too soft). We reject a stick of wood (no thin edge). We reject a spade (too heavy and unwieldy). We look for a screwdriver (just right). The criterion here is *agreement* between the requirements of the needed tool and the properties of a screwdriver.

Another important criterion for judgment is *logical consistency*. Are two items of information compatible? Contradiction between two items is sufficient grounds for rejection, as when a conclusion cannot follow from a given fact. Actually, the criteria of identity, agreement, and consistency are all logical criteria, in a broad conception of "logical." This view is in keeping with the general principle that intellectual functioning is by nature logical.

EVALUATION OF UNITS

Visual Units (EVU)

Most known tasks for *EVU* that have been used as tests employ the criterion of identity. In effect, they ask, "Is this figure exactly the same as that one?" as in the items in *Figure 8.1*. The objects are radios that differ very little from one another. For each radio at the left there is a matching radio at the right. Which lettered radio matches each numbered radio? Differences occur in some having rounded corners and some square ones, in length of foundation piece, and in organization of white lines over the speaker at the left. For items *1* through *4* the correct matches are *B, C, A,* and *D.*

Figure 8.1

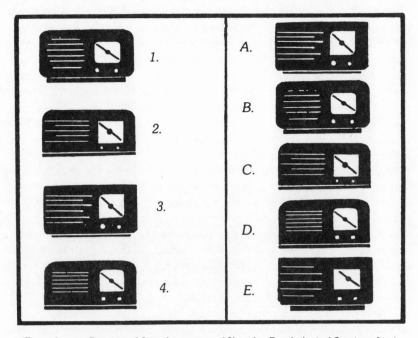

(From the test *Perceptual Speed,* courtesy of Sheridan Psychological Services, Inc.)

Something can be said concerning places in which ability *EVU* has been found relevant. An example is found in certain factories that make fabrics and clothing. Inspectors of the output of products would depend significantly on *EVU,* or those who match articles, such as socks or stockings.

Auditory Units (EAU)

Ability *EAU* was found in a special investigation of abilities that are relevant in the early stages of learning to read. The beginner in reading must be quite sure about what he hears, for he depends upon fine distinctions in speech sounds in association with printed words. For example, he must cognize that the word "rug" is not the same as "tug" or "bug," in which only one phoneme differs. He must distinguish words with "S" sounds, as in the pairs "fix" and "six" or "foe" and "so." Mastering such discriminations helps him to make parallel differentiations in printed words.

Symbolic Units (ESU)

The criterion of identity is very commonly used in a task of comparisons of letter and number combinations. In the following pairs of symbolic units you are to judge whether the two members are the same or different, and to write S or D, respectively, in the blank spaces.

52163	_____	52163
7ap4υ	_____	7ap4υ
difference	_____	differance
Hahn, Lorena	_____	Hahn, Lorina
NXOYM	_____	NXOYM

If you had enough time, you could, of course, get all these items right. But only a short time is allowed and you have to work rapidly to make a good score. This kind of task is popular in tests for clerical aptitude, for a clerk or typist must work rapidly and must detect very small differences and mistakes in printed material. The case of the proofreader was mentioned earlier.

The second illustrative task is given because it utilizes the criterion of agreement with specifications. In the following list of words, check every word that contains the letter U:

( ) sense	( ) contour	( ) spice
( ) juice	( ) long	( ) elude
( ) special	( ) frank	( ) ground

This test is also given with a short working time. Although it may not appear on its surface to have the same potential usefulness as the one just mentioned because it measures the same *ESU* ability, it could serve the same purposes.

Semantic Units (EMU)

A task that represents *EMU* is similar in form to that of the "letter-U" test just described for *ESU*. Among the following objects check those that are both round and hard:

( ) copper	( ) doughnut	( ) ball bearing
( ) camera	( ) muffin	( ) phonograph record
( ) coin	( ) pill	( ) meatball

Some of these objects are round but not hard while others are hard but not round. Only those that have both attributes satisfy the specifications.

In everyday life we usually have to set up our own specifications, but they are often implied by the problem as we understand it. A test called *Object Synthesis* is used to illustrate ability *NMT*. In it, you have to say what object could be reasonably made by combining two other given objects. In doing this test, you would probably evaluate the answers you think of before reporting them. The scorer who judges your answers is engaging in evaluation, particularly the ability *EMU*. He is judging the suitability of the objects you give for serving the purpose. This activity is utilized in a test for *EMU*. Each item presents two objects and three alternative objects each of which could possibly be made from them. The test item asks you to say which is the best answer and which is the worst. Here are three items:

Given objects:	Alternative answers:
1. lace curtain	A. Christmas wrapping
wire hanger	B. mop
	C. butterfly net
2. wax paper	A. book cover
glue	B. paper cup
	C. doll
3. wire screen	A. basketball goal
barrel hoop	B. sand sifter
	C. bird cage

The "right" answers to such items are sometimes debatable, but for testing purposes a scoring key can be established. The key for these three items is as follows:

> 1. C is best; A poorest.
> 2. C is best; B poorest.
> 3. B is best; A poorest.

It should be noted that in this test some relative judgments have been introduced, in that the three alternative answers are *ranked*. In the other illustrations thus far the judgments have been absolute; the suggested response will do or it will not do. In evaluations, decisions can be simply *yes* or *no* or they can be on a scale of goodness.

In the next example for *EMU* the criterion for judgment is consistency. Each item is a sentence with two parts. Sometimes the two parts are consistent, sometimes not. In which of the following sentences are there inconsistencies?

> 1. *Johnny, who is seven, went to Europe with his
> mother ten years ago.*

2. *He finished the note in pencil because his pen had
   run out of ink.*

3. *The soldier preferred being a coward to becoming
   a corpse for the rest of his life.*

Decisions are easy to make as to which particular sentences are nonsensical because of internal inconsistencies. Units are evaluated because it is ideas that are compared.

EVALUATION OF CLASSES

Judgments pertaining to classes are of several kinds. We can ask whether a certain class name or description fits a set of similar items of information, or which of several names fits best. We can ask whether a given item belongs to a certain class, or we can ask to which class it best belongs. Or, we can ask whether two items have enough similarity to belong to the same class. These kinds of evaluative decisions will be illustrated in the tasks described in this section.

Visual Classes (EVC)

Figure 8.2 presents a typical task applied for *EVC*. Four selected figural classes are named by giving the common feature in each case — right angles, parallel lines, similar shape, and open figures. These classes have just been mentioned in the order of importance assigned to them, as in the illustration. Each test problem contains three pairs of figures, *A, B,* and *C.* The pair in each case could represent one or more classes. The problem is to select the pair that belongs in the most valuable class.

In problem *1,* the best we can do is to choose answer *C,* in which there are two similar angles, which puts them in class three, the case of similar shapes. In problem 2, we find nothing better than two open figures (answer *C*), so they go with the least important class. In item *3* we can do better, for members of the *B* pair have parallel lines, like the pair in the second class. The pair of crescents (answer *A*) would qualify for the third class, but we do better by choosing pair *B.*

Symbolic Classes (ESC)

For *ESC* we utilize a task very similar to the one just described for *EVC.* The ranked classes, from best to poorest, are:

1. *perfect squares*
2. *multiples of some number*
3. *odd numbers or even numbers*
4. *all other classes*

Figure 8.2

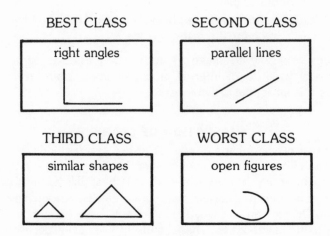

BEST CLASS

right angles

SECOND CLASS

parallel lines

THIRD CLASS

similar shapes

WORST CLASS

open figures

PROBLEMS

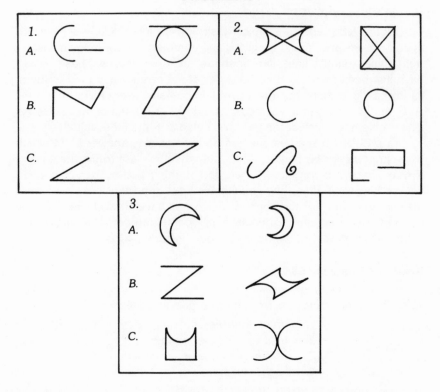

What are the highest-ranking pairs in each of the following items?

1. A. 2 - 7	2. A. 3 - 6	3. A. 6 - 4
B. 5 - 2	B. 6 - 5	B. 4 - 9
C. 7 - 5	C. 5 - 3	C. 9 - 6

The right answers are C, A, and B, for which the reasons should be fairly obvious. These are the highest-ranking classes for the pairs of numbers in the same item.

Semantic Classes (EMC)

Finding the best class label, selected from alternatives, is the nature of the first task illustrating *EMC*. Most objects are members of several classes, broad and narrow. For each of the following given objects, which is the most descriptive or definitive class label?

1. PALM	A. plant	B. tree
	C. branch	D. leaf
2. DENTIST	A. job	B. occupation
	C. profession	D. position
3. SHIRT	A. garment	B. fashion
	C. decoration	D. covering
4. ORANGE	A. juice	B. fruit
	C. tree	D. flavor

With a little stretch of the imagination, more than one alternative is a possible answer in some of these items, but one of them is most descriptive. If you could name only one of the classes to help convey to a friend the most information regarding the object, which would it be? The keyed answers are: *B, C, A,* and *B.*

The second illustration for *EMC* is a task that asks which word among four alternatives has the most in common with the given word, hence is best classified with it. The words and alternatives are:

1. FATHER	A. candidate	B. umpire
	C. superintendent	D. salesman
2. MISER	A. butcher	B. banker
	C. farmer	D. postman
3. CHILD	A. calf	B. pet
	C. elf	D. human
4. SALESMAN	A. teller	B. preacher
	C. draftsman	D. secretary

Some of the alternatives are rather remote but it is possible to find attributes in common. The question is, which pairs — given object and alternative — have the most in common? The keyed answers are: *C, B, A,* and *B.*

EVALUATION OF RELATIONS

In other mental-operation categories you have seen that the favorite kinds of tasks involving relations are either analogy or trend tests. The same kinds of tests are adaptable also to the evaluation area. One kind of item calls for the best analogy among alternatives in order to match a given relationship. One is a closer duplicate than the others. In other tests using several alternatives, none duplicates the given relationship exactly but one comes nearest to matching. Both kinds call for a ranking of alternatives.

Visual Relations (EVR)

In one figural-relations-evaluation task you are told what the relation or relations are, and you are to find among alternatives the figure that satisfies each specified relation, as in *Figure 8.3*. In one item you are told that related to the given figure is another that is an inversion and that the circle is smaller. Among the alternative answers, *B* fulfills these specifications. Both relations have been satisfied, whereas in others one or both relations are missing.

Figure 8.3

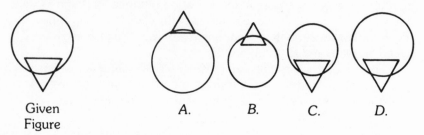

Given   A.   B.   C.   D.
Figure

Symbolic Relations (ESR)

In an analogies task for *ESR*, a pair of related words is given, followed by three alternative pairs of words. One of these pairs has a relation that can be regarded as *most nearly* like that for the given pair. Some sample items are:

Given pairs:	Alternative pairs:
1. *GRAND-RAN*	A. *country-cot* B. *respite-sit*
	C. *loving-log*

2. *LIST-LOST*   A. *rag-rug*   B. *tare-tire*
                     C. *cell-cull*

3. *REAL-SEAL*   A. *fast-last*   B. *tore-sore*
                     C. *sent-tent*

4. *RINSING-GRIN*   A. *aprons-sap*   B. *earth-hear*
                     C. *estimate-test*

The keyed answers, with reasons, are:

1. B *("Sit" is composed only of central letters of "respite.")*
2. B *(Other pairs of vowels are farther apart in the alphabet.)*
3. C *(Initial letters are in direct alphabetical order.)*
4. B *(Second word is formed from last letter and first three letters of the first word.)*

As stated earlier, some items have no completely correct alternatives; only a best alternative. This variation applies in items 1 and 2 here.

Semantic Relations (EMC)

There is a semantic test completely parallel in format to the symbolic one just described. Again, some fine distinctions must be made among alternatives. Here are a few items:

    Given pairs: *Alternative pairs:*

1. *BIRD-SONG*   A. *fish-swim*   B. *man-letter*
                     C. *pianist-piano*

2. *FISH-WORM*   A. *pole-hook*   B. *crumb-bird*
                     C. *fire-wood*

3. *PENCIL-PEN*   A. *hill-lake*   B. *chalk-paint*
                     C. *writing-print*

4. *BUY-SELL*   A. *catch-throw*   B. *found-lost*
                     C. *steal-pawn*

Some of the parallels between the given and alternative pairs are not very easy to see, and some wrong alternatives may look tempting. The following matches should be made:

1. B *(Man produces a letter as bird produces song.)*
2. C *(Fire consumes wood as fish consumes worm.)*
3. B *(Chalk and paint are also dry and wet writing materials.*
4. A *(Catch and throw mean receiving versus parting with something, like buy and sell.)*

For some reason, ability *EMR* has been found related to achievement in 9th-grade algebra. Presumably, this could be due to some
semantic relations that the student encounters and uses, and that he has
to evaluate, for example, "equality" and "inequality," "powers" and
"roots." His success depends in part upon how well he applies these
concepts; how well he finds that they apply as well as do not apply.

EVALUATION OF SYSTEMS

As in connection with other products, the evaluation of systems is
concerned with satisfaction of specifications. In other instances, it also
emphasizes the criterion of consistency, mainly internal consistency. All
of these cases will be seen in the illustrations to be given.

Visual Systems (EVS)

In the test *Judging Figural Balance,* which is illustrated in *Figure 8.4,*
the task is to say which of three defined kinds of balance each figural
system satisfies. A symmetrical system *(A)* is a case of bilateral
symmetry. A vertical straight line drawn down the middle would divide
the total area so that one half is a mirror image of the other. The case of
informal balance *(B)* has equal weights of objects on either side but no
mirror image. Conditions are a little relaxed in that if the division line
were drawn somewhat off the vertical, matched objects would still be on
either side. In the case of complete balance *(C)* we could draw a straight
line anywhere across the square and find equal amounts of shaded area
on either side of it.

What kinds of systems appear in items *1* through *3?* Item *1* is of
the informal type; item *2* belongs in the symmetrical category; and item
3 has complete balance. In this test it can be said that there are three
specified systems, and the task is to match given systems with those
specifications.

Symbolic Systems (ESS)

Number systems and letter systems can also be used in measuring
symbolic-evaluation abilities. One task presents the principle that applies
to letter series, and lists a group of series some of which follow the
principle and some do not. Suppose the principle were "alternate letters
of the alphabet." Which of the following series conform to that
specification?

1. *M O Q S U W*
2. *C E G I K M*
3. *P R S U W Y*

Figure 8.4

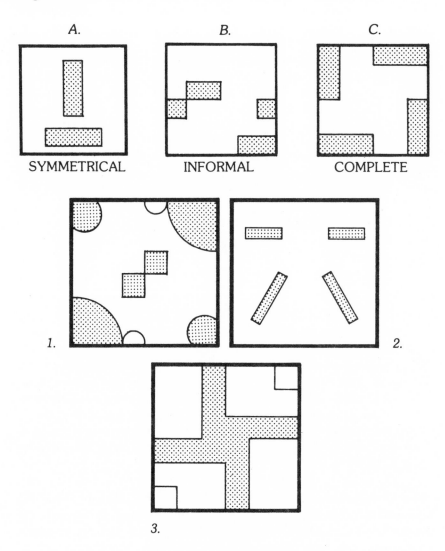

4. *J L N P R T*
5. *A C E H J L*

Examination of these series will show that series *1, 2,* and *4* do conform to the principle of skipping one letter while *3* and *5* do not.

The relevance of *ESS* for mathematics is obvious. One needs to check expressions and equations almost constantly.

Semantic Systems (EMS)

You have previously seen problems of the type that ask, "What is wrong with this picture?" The things that are wrong are incongruent either with other things in the picture or with what is known from previous experience. *Figure 8.5* presents a problem of this type, with a clock and a lamp on a table. The test *Unlikely Things* does not simply ask the question quoted above. Instead, it names four things that are actually wrong in the picture and you are to select the two things that are most seriously wrong. The four errors to be seen in the picture in *Figure 8.5*, which would appear along with the picture in a test problem are:

1. *The hands of the clock are of the same length.*
2. *The light is shining, yet the lamp cord is not plugged in.*
3. *The end of the lamp cord has no prongs for plugging in.*
4. *Some numbers on the clock are out of order.*

The question to be answered in this test is: *Which two things are "most" unusual?* Which two stated defects or errors are less likely to occur? The keyed answers to the given item are 2 and 4. It would be possible for an amateur electrician to put the wrong plug at the end of the lamp cord. It would be possible for a clock assembler to get two hands of the same length on the same clock face. It is not so likely that printed numbers would get out of order on a clock face, and impossible for an ordinary electric light bulb to shine without being plugged in.

If you ask which people are involved with *EMS* activities very heavily, the answer is, "All of us." Individuals who are most generally dependent upon *EMS* include those who serve in the capacity of critics of either spoken or written discourse. This includes speakers and writers who judge their own products, as well as teachers who read compositions and answers to examination questions involving organized thinking. It includes those who judge the soundness of scientific theories or the workability of organized plans of operation. And let us not forget judges and trial juries, who must decide the guilt or innocence of a defendant, or the rights in a civil case. Men and women of recognized wisdom are probably high in *EMS*.

Figure 8.5

EVALUATION OF TRANSFORMATIONS

Sometimes when transformations occur, they are designed to serve certain purposes. In such cases, our judgment is whether or not, or how well, the change has served the intended purpose. Another occasion for judgment in this product area is to decide how much of a change has occurred, or whether or not any change has occurred at all. Sometimes we need to decide whether or not a certain outcome has been merely a change of a certain kind. It may be some other kind of instance.

Visual Transformations (EVT)

Movement of something in space is one of the most common transformations of a visual nature. In tests for *EVT* we can use pictured objects, such as an alarm clock, shown in a starting position, along with some alternative views of the clock in different positions. We can ask in which of the alternative positions has the clock undergone the most movement.

A different kind of test is shown in *Figure 8.6*. At the top a certain figure is shown, divided into parts. In the items below it, which figures could have been made simply by rearrangement of the four parts of the top figure? Inspection of the item figures should show that only the one in item 4 could not be made by such rearranging. The rearranging is the transformation, which is being judged.

Figure 8.6

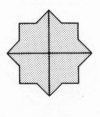

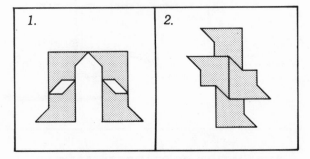

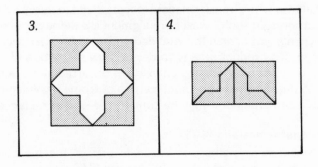

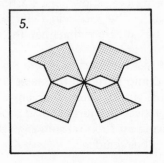

Symbolic Transformations (EST)

One illustrative test for *EST* here makes use of rearrangements of letters within words as transformations. In the test *Jumbled Words*, for each given word, five other words are also given. Some of the latter can be made merely by rearranging the letters of the word given first and some not. Here are a couple of items:

1. *PURSE*   A. *sprue*   B. *super*   C. *reuse*
               D. *puree*   E. *upper*

2. *STREAM*   A. *merits*   B. *master*   C. *smarts*
                 D. *tamers*   E. *steams*

In yes-no decisions it is easy to see that in item *1* the correct transformations occur in words *A* and *B;* in item 2, they are in words *B* and *D*.

Operations in ordinary algebra call for transformations on every hand, so it is easy to find problems for a test for *EST,* provided the examinees have had at least high-school algebra. The format of the test is like the one in the test just described, with a starting expression and several alternative potential transformations for yes-no decisions; results are correct transforms or they are not. For one problem the given expression is:

$$\frac{2x + 4y}{8x}$$

The suggested alternative transforms are:

A. $\dfrac{2(x + 2y)}{8x}$ B. $\dfrac{4(x + y)}{8x}$ C. $\dfrac{1}{4x}\left(\dfrac{x}{2} + y \right)$

D. $\dfrac{x + 2y}{4x}$ E. $\dfrac{4(x/2 + y)}{8x}$

Correct transformations are found in alternatives *A, D,* and *E;* not in *B* and *C.*

From superficial examination of these two tests for *EST* it would not be obvious that they both measure the same ability. But this is the case, as factor analysis shows. Psychologically they have an underlying common function involved. It would thus be possible to measure at least this aspect of aptitude for algebra with students who have had no algebra, by giving the *Jumbled Words* test.

The more general significance of this illustration is that if we know or have good reason to believe that a certain *Structure-of-Intellect* ability is a component of achievement in any subject or skill, we can assess that particular component by using test material that is adapted to the examinees before their actual learning in the subject or skill. This is the principle on which all aptitude tests should rest.

Semantic Transformations (EMT)

Tests for *EMT* have typically asked the examinee to say which of two or more statements involves a transformation, or, if all statements do so, it asks for judgments of more or less transformation. One test is based upon cartoon pictures, such as that in *Figure 8.7*. A man is sitting at a table in a restaurant. He is angrily pointing at a sign under a hatrack as a waiter stands nearby. Below his hat the sign reads "Watch your hat." Below the cartoon are pairs of statements that the man might be saying to the waiter. Three of these pairs read:

1. A. *My hat is old enough to watch itself.*
   B. *I've watched it so long it's last year's model.*
2. A. *You thought I wouldn't see the fly in my soup.*
   B. *My hat's all right, but where is my steak?*
3. A. *Do you think I have eyes in the back of my head?*
   B. *While I was watching my hat, someone stole my coat.*

In each of these items, which statement is more unexpected, out of the ordinary, more funny, or more clever? These are ways of asking, "Which one involves more of a transformation?" For item *1, A* is the better answer because the hat is transformed into something more human-like. For item *2, A* is also the keyed answer. It changes the intention of the sign. As for item *3*, statement *A* is just a sarcastic remark, but *B* brings in an entirely unexpected turn of events, hence is the accepted answer for a scoring point.

Recall from earlier chapters the connection pointed out between transformations and humor. That connection is quite evident in the *Punch-Line Comparisons* test that we have just been considering. In connection with the use of plot-titles tests mentioned in *Chapter 6*, for the assessment of the parallel ability *DMT*, only clever responses are counted toward the total score. It is assumed that clever titles as well as clever comments involve transformations. The scorer who decides whether or not a response is clever is making judgments like those involved in the test just described. It is hoped that the scorer ranks high with respect to *EMT*.

EVALUATIONS OF IMPLICATIONS

Since implications are projections or conclusions from given information, and since several implications can often be found to follow from the same source, there is considerable room for both correct and

Figure 8.7

incorrect answers. Some implications are more sound or more justified than others, and it takes good judgment to tell the difference.

Visual Implications (EVI)

The illustrative task for *EVI* uses *Figure 8.8,* in which you see a simple maze. There are four problems, involving routes to be taken in going from the numbered points at the corners of the maze to the black goal in the center. Several lettered points appear at places within the pathways in the maze. The problem is to decide through which of these points one *must* pass in order to reach the goal, following the lines from the numbered starting point.

From point number *1* you could go through either point *A* or point *C*, but you must go through point *D*, which is therefore the right answer. Starting at point *2*, you could go through either *B* or *H*, but point *E* is a must. Necessary points when starting from *3* or *4* are *G* and *D*, respectively. In each problem the nature of the paths implies the route to the goal.

Figure 8.8

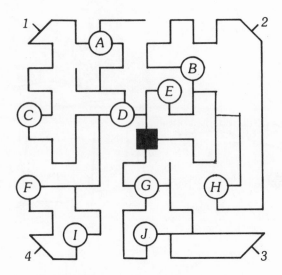

(Adapted from an Air Force experimental test.)

Symbolic Implications (ESI)

Abbreviations are in very common use these days, especially with the government inventing new organizations with long names. Have you tried to figure out what a new abbreviation stands for? You may think of several possibilities (divergent production), then you have the task of deciding which one is the most likely (evaluation). The illustrative *ESI* test is based upon a similar task. You are given an abbreviation and three alternative words for which it might stand. Which one is the most likely? Some items are:

1. *CRNT*   A. *crescent*   B. *coronation*
              C. *current*

2. *RCTN*   A. *reaction*   B. *relation*
              C. *recreation*

3. *DARG*   A. *danger*   B. *daring*
              C. *darning*

If you try to pronounce the abbreviation it will help decide which word it stands for. In this task the abbreviation implies the word and you make a relative judgment. The best answers for items *1* through *3* are *C*, *A*, and *B*.

Semantic Implications (EMI)

A variety of tasks could be cited to represent ability *EMI*. First, there are some involving syllogisms. In the preceding chapter you saw how a syllogism test in *completion* form can be used to assess the parallel ability *NMI*. For an evaluation test for *EMI* we should have to use a true-false or a multiple-choice form. In either case conclusions are also given to be judged.

Actually, it is not necessary to present two premises, because conclusions can be drawn from single statements. That approach is used in one task for *EMI*. In the *Sentence Selection* test, a statement of fact is given. Following it are several items, each containing three possible conclusions, one of which follows logically from the statement. Which is the justified conclusion in each of the items following this statement?

> *Statement: A student who helped a friend during an important examination was accused of cheating, which led to his being expelled from college.*

1. A. *Cheaters are often found out.*
   B. *Some colleges consider cheating a serious offense.*
   C. *Tests should be given individually to prevent cheating.*

2. A. *Helping friends sometimes gets one into trouble.*
   B. *Since the college could not prove that he cheated, it shouldn't have expelled him.*
   C. *The rate of cheating at the college was decreased.*

3. A. The college had a very strict honor system.
    B. The teacher was negligent to let such a thing happen.
    C. Helping another to cheat is sometimes regarded as bad as cheating itself.

In selecting the best conclusion in each item of this test, you have to be sure that it does follow from the given statement. Other given conclusions may well state true facts when considered by themselves, but there is not sufficient information given to justify them. They have to rest on knowledge from other sources. With these restrictions in mind, the best, in fact the only correct conclusions, are B, A, and C.

In the next illustrative task for EMI, you are given first in each problem the name of an object. Each object implies a number of things associated with it. Four of the associated things are given as alternative answers to each item. Which of the four is *always* required by the given object; something that it could not exist or function without?

1. BOOK	A. words	B. pages
	C. pictures	D. story
2. RADIO PROGRAM	A. announcer	B. sponsor
	C. sound	D. commercial
3. ALARM CLOCK	A. wakening	B. electricity
	C. signal	D. bedroom
4. LEADER	A. power	B. follower
	C. prestige	D. enemy
5. CIRCUS	A. performers	B. audience
	C. tent	D. animals

Perhaps the right answers to these items need some explaining. A *book* must have *pages* or it would not be a book; they might even all be blank. A *radio program* is made to transmit *sounds*, whatever else it may do. An *alarm clock* has a *signal*, or at least a mechanism for one; that is its unique feature. A *leader* is not justifiably called that unless he has at least one *follower*. A *circus* is not a circus without *performers*, for entertainment is its purpose.

EMI is concerned in much of the area of critical thinking, which can now be much better defined. It can prevent us from being gullible; from believing everything we hear or read. Courses in formal logic were said to be offered to teach students how to test propositions as to their validity. A much broader approach toward the same goal would be to realize what it is that needs to be judged and what the criteria for evaluation are. What needs to be judged are the products of information in all the content areas. The criteria illustrated in this chapter were identity, agreement, and consistency. Formal logic is very much confined to semantic and symbolic information, to the product of implication, and the criterion of consistency. The broader approach would involve exercises in all kinds of information, with all kinds of criteria.

WHAT EVALUATION ABILITIES DO NOT COVER

In everyday life, we indulge in many kinds of judgments that are not represented among the evaluative abilities included in the domain of intelligence. At the opening of this chapter some examples were cited from our motor activity, in which muscular movements are checked and either corrected or allowed to continue as they are. Even within the *Structure-of-Intellect* model, only one auditory-evaluation ability was mentioned, and no behavioral-evaluation abilities were treated because of the lack of investigation within those two content areas.

You might well ask, "What about aesthetic and ethical judgments?" "Are they within the intellectual realm or are they outside?" We can say with some confidence that aesthetic judgments, as they apply to visual items of information, do not come within the intellectual realm. Tests that call for aesthetic judgments do not correlate with tests calling for logical judgments, as for intellectual abilities. The reason is probably that there are no logical criteria that apply to aesthetic experiences. We still have no information regarding aesthetic judgments in other content areas — auditory and semantic, for example. Music and literature fall within these areas.

As for ethical judgments, there would seem to be a better chance of applying at least quasi-standards that would be effective. But agreed-upon moral standards would need to be established. Legal standards are much better defined, with logical criteria being applicable. Legal matters also include behavioral information, such as items of motivation and intention. Judgments in these areas would be in the category of behavioral evaluation.

SUMMARY

The operation of evaluation is concerned with decisions about the goodness of items of information. It involves checking on the information that we have, however it came about, and making decisions or rendering judgments regarding it. It is a way of telling us whether we are on the right track and should continue or whether we are wrong or could do better. In the latter case some change of direction or some correction is called for. Evaluation is the area of critical thinking.

In making decisions regarding goodness, some criteria for judgment are needed. Investigations of evaluative abilities have shown what some of those criteria are. Criteria that apply to all kinds of products of information involve identity, which requires comparisons of items in order to determine whether they are exactly the same, or which pairs of items are more nearly the same. The judgments may be relative as well as absolute.

Another quite general criterion is whether an item of information conforms to specifications or requirements that are given to us or that are implied by the situation. Suitability of a given object to serve a certain purpose comes in this particular category. Still another common criterion is consistency. This may mean consistency or compatibility between items of information or it may mean internal consistency, as in systems.

Certain product categories have some special criteria that apply more obviously to them. In connection with classes we may ask what is the best classification for an object, where several alternative classifications are logical. Or, given a set of objects clearly belonging to a class, what is the best class description? The same question can be asked regarding a relation that we encounter. In connection with transformations we may ask whether or not one has occurred, or, of two given transformations which one is a greater change.

Because of our tendency to check all information processing, evaluative abilities have almost as wide application as cognitive abilities. Because criteria for evaluation are logical in nature, the intellectual abilities probably do not apply to aesthetic and ethical judgments. We already know that they do not apply to judgments of certain aesthetic qualities of visual figures.

CHAPTER NINE

The Structure of Intellect

At the end of *Chapter 3* you were introduced to the information matrix, a model in two dimensions to represent different kinds of content and kinds of products. We can now bring the different kinds of operations into the picture simply by adding a third dimension. The result is shown in *Figure 9.1*—the *Structure-of-Intellect* model.

Figure 9.1

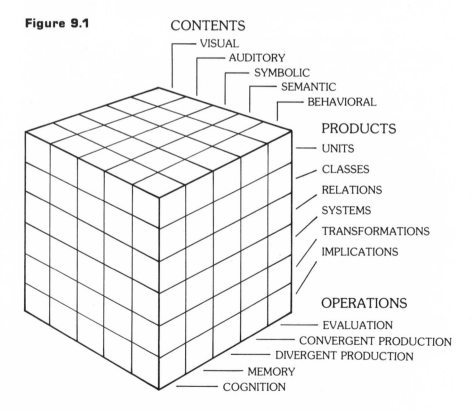

CONTENTS
- VISUAL
- AUDITORY
- SYMBOLIC
- SEMANTIC
- BEHAVIORAL

PRODUCTS
- UNITS
- CLASSES
- RELATIONS
- SYSTEMS
- TRANSFORMATIONS
- IMPLICATIONS

OPERATIONS
- EVALUATION
- CONVERGENT PRODUCTION
- DIVERGENT PRODUCTION
- MEMORY
- COGNITION

Each little cube or cell in the model stands for one particular intellectual ability or function. As you have seen in the preceding chapters, each ability is defined by a conjunction of three categories — operation with content with product — denoted by its trigram symbol. With five kinds of operations, five kinds of contents, and six kinds of products, 5 × 5 × 6 yields 150 possible unique abilities, of which more than two-thirds have been demonstrated by factor analysis. The remainder seem not to have been investigated. As you have already seen in the preceding chapters, the latter are almost entirely in the auditory and behavioral categories.

In view of the general appearance of the model some facetious remarks have been made. One student summed it up by saying, "This model shows what I have always suspected; we are all blockheads." Another remarked that the model means that mentally we are all squares. Still another offered the observation, "So *this* is our mental block!" It is, indeed, one of our mental blocks; a most important one.

ORDERS AMONG THE CATEGORIES

There is more meaningfulness about the model than just some classifications. The order of the categories within each dimension of the model was chosen with some.thought to their logical interrelationships.

The order of the content categories puts figural (visual and auditory) abilities first, in recognition of the fact that perceived information is nearest to the step of input from the environment and the fact that other kinds of information are ultimately derived from figural information. Symbolic is not very far removed from figural information. In fact, you have seen how letters and numbers can be used in either way in figural and symbolic tests. The connection of symbolic information to semantic information is seen in the fact that the former labels and communicates the latter quite generally. When we come to behavioral information, however, order is not so clear, for it has ready connections with both semantic and figural information. It would not be reasonable to place behavioral information first. A possible solution would be to make the content dimension circular, with behavioral information next to both its neighbors.

Among the kinds of operations, cognition is basic, as we have seen on a number of occasions. Other operations depend upon it in a natural sequence: cognition (structuring information), memory (putting items into storage), and then productive thinking (with retrieval of information from storage), including divergent production (broad search) and convergent production (focused search). Evaluation has relations with all other kinds of operation, since items derived either from cognition or from productive thinking are likely to be evaluated. But it occurs after each of the other operations in time and for that reason is placed last in line.

As for relations among the kinds of products, it has been pointed out that units are basic because they can not only form connections with one another but also play roles in all other kinds of products. Units almost automatically have class memberships, so classes are next in the model. Units are connected two at a time by relations, a relatively simple kind of connection. Three or more units in certain relationships form a system, the most complex kind of item. Transformations and implications are put last because, in the first case an item undergoes changes to become something else, and in the second case an implied item follows from another item.

SI ABILITIES AND THE IQ

Having this extensive system of human intellectual abilities with which to work, as provided by the *SI* model, we are in a good position to examine some common IQ scales in order to see what they represent in the way of coverage of intelligence. This exercise is very important in view of the many claims that are made these days, particularly regarding racial and ethnical differences in "intelligence."

Such claims are relevant only to whatever abilities are assessed by the IQ scales that have been used. A thorough and enlightened investigation of any group differences would be made in terms of measurement with tests of known *SI* coverage. In evaluating the findings and conclusions thus far reported, it should be helpful to know just what kind of sampling of abilities the utilized IQ scales have provided. It has often been realized that IQ tests do fall short of covering the whole range of intellectual talents, but the actual shortage has not heretofore been known.

SI Abilities Represented in the Stanford-Binet Scale

The *Stanford-Binet Scale* includes 140 test problems tailored for different levels of mental maturity. Each tested individual would be administered only a fraction of these problems, those near his mental-age level. Excluded would be problems at year levels above the one at which he fails all items and also those at levels below which he passes all items. Thus, he may be administered perhaps about 25 of the 140 problems.

Among the total 140 problems it has been estimated that as many as

28 *SI* abilities are represented each by at least one problem. At any one age level, of course, with only seven problems, only a few *SI* abilities could be covered. Another limitation is that different *SI* abilities are represented at different age levels, to some extent on a hit-or-miss basis.

A very few *SI* abilities are represented from one year level to the next. The three most often appearing thus are abilities *CMU, CMS,* and *MSS.* The first two of these are important in reading comprehension and the third is involved in rote memory of number series, as in memory-span tests. IQ tests were designed to indicate aptitude for learning in elementary school work, hence these emphases are understandable.

In order to be a little more systematic about the matter, let us see how well different dimensions of the *SI* model are covered in the *Stanford* scale. As to operations, cognition and memory are overwhelmingly represented. There is a little on convergent production and evaluation, but virtually nothing on divergent production. As to informational content, semantic abilities dominate the scene, with less attention to symbolic content, and nothing on either behavioral or auditory content. The products most emphasized are units and systems, with no attention given, at least directly, to classes. Because of the common utility of classes, the latter oversight would seem to be serious.

Other Intelligence Scales

Other standard IQ scales, such as Wechsler's, the *Lorge-Thorndike,* and the *California Test of Mental Maturity,* have tended to turn assessment of intelligence somewhat in different directions. But even so, all scales fall very short of covering the whole territory. It is important, also, to remember that each scale tends to make a somewhat different sampling of *SI* abilities, so that IQs from one scale do not represent the same aspects of intelligence as do others.

A general conclusion is that an IQ that would assess all of intelligence would have to go beyond any that now exist — way beyond. Another general conclusion is that a single composite score like an IQ, although very appealing because of its utter simplicity, is not the way to describe the intellectual status of individuals. Even two composite scores, as a verbal and nonverbal IQ, would fall short and would suffer the disadvantage of all composite scores — the loss of information because of ambiguity. What is needed is a profile of scores, in which the individual's strengths and weaknesses are displayed. The profile need not include all 150 components, for in most cases there would be interest in a selected combination of *SI* abilities, for use in a particular situation. All this envisages an effective, if somewhat elaborate, aptitude-testing technology. The payoff in terms of educational and vocational guidance should be very substantial.

SUMMARY

The *Structure-of-Intellect* model is a three-way classification of known and conceivable human intellectual abilities or functions, represented by a three-dimensional cubic design. Each dimension includes a set of categories, one for five kinds of operation, one for five kinds of informational content, and one for six kinds of products. Each ability is represented by a single cell, with its unique conjunction of three values on the three dimensions. Certain psychological relations determine the order of categories along each dimension.

The model not only brings into focus the numerous shortcomings of present standard ways of assessing intelligence of individuals but also presents vistas of the way toward a fuller and more meaningful description of their intellectual status.

EXERCISES

A list of activities is presented below in order that you may test yourself, if you so desire, as to how well you can recognize the roles of intellectual ability and functioning. You will need to discriminate among kinds of operation, content, and product in each case.

Each problem describes or illustrates a kind of activity, and you are to decide which *SI* ability is prominently involved. It should be said that the operation of cognition is naturally involved in all of them. You should name an ability in the cognition category only when no other kind of operation is apparent. List your answers in the form of the trigram symbols for the abilities. If you think that two abilities are prominently involved, include both in your answer.

Problems:

1. What do we call the "boss" of a football team during a game? (Just as an example, the answer to this problem should be *NMU* — the "naming" ability mentioned in *Chapter 7*.)
2. Memorize the telephone number: 213 475 0285.
3. How many meanings do you see for the word "fly"?
4. Make up several puns using the word "tooth."
5. You find a comic strip amusing.
6. Simplify the expression: $5(x + 2y) - 2(2x + y)$.
7. You first thought the man was angry, but on looking more closely you decided that he was disgusted.
8. Looking at the road map, you see that the most direct route is through Mudville.

9. Seeing a crowd of people gathered near some cars stopped on a highway, you think that an accident has occurred.

10. You suggest several ideas for advertising a play that your group is soon to put on.

11. You group children whom you are studying according to sex, age, and ethnic origin.

12. In how many ways could you combine coins to add up to 30 cents?

13. You make up some "wise cracks" to amuse your friends.

14. If X + Y = A and A - B = Y, what does X equal?

15. Is this short melody exactly the same as that one?

16. OUT is to IN as DAY is to which of these: A. week   B. night C. daylight   D. morning?

17. Since the possessive of "he" is "his," logically, the possessive of "she" should be what?

18. An angry-looking girl is pointing her finger at her cringing younger brother, from which you get the impression that she is accusing him of something.

19. Make the capital letter M, with an upside-down M on top of it and touching it.

20. How would you describe the principle of this number series: 3, 6, 7, 14, 15, 30?

21. After you have taken a series of ten tests in succession, you are given the names of the tests in scrambled order and you are told to say which came first, second, third, etc.

22. You learn and remember the arrangement of streets and houses in a neighborhood to which you have moved.

23. You read and understand a paragraph of an essay.

24. Make a list of all the things that you think are impossible.

25. What object is meant by each of the following figurative descriptions:
Men playing ball with a foot
A piece of furniture copying notes
A lawn jumping about

26. You solve this problem: Two men applied for a job. Their last names were the same, and it was discovered that they were brothers. They gave the same date of birth and the same parents. Yet, when asked about it, they declared that they were not twins.[1]

27. You decide which one of several stated facts is not needed in

---

[1] The men were two among triplets.

order to solve a certain arithmetical problem.

28. Is this line of thinking correct? All haystacks are catfish, and all catfish are typewriters, therefore, all haystacks are typewriters.

29. You learn which friend's name goes with which telephone number in your "little black book."

30. You solve this problem: Given a board 3 feet wide and 8 feet long, show how by cutting it into 2 pieces you could make a board 2 feet wide and 12 feet long by joining them.

31. You learn to recognize a certain vase when you see it again.

32. By rearranging letters, make another word out of SHAH.

33. If you see a man beating a child, what different conclusions could you draw?

34. You are driving in a fog and you are not sure whether the object in the road ahead is a cow or a truck. You decide it is a truck.

35. What difficulties do you foresee in training a dog?

36. You are piloting a small airplane and you see the horizon and the ground at one side of it, from which you know the posture of the plane and the direction in which it is going.

37. What are these garbled words: TCA   MABLER   AHRHS.

38. What is absurd about this statement: Mrs. Smith had no children, and I understand the same was true of her mother.

39. Write a list of four-letter words that end in N.

40. From all the evidence the jury decided that the man intended to commit the murder.

Answers to problems:

Although it is true that the *SI* ability that is most prominent in each given activity depends somewhat upon the circumstances, we shall assume that the conditions for those activities are not unusual. If you do not agree with the keyed best answers given below, reexamine the stated activity and try to see the reasons why that particular ability is listed. When a second ability is notably involved it is stated in the key.

1. *NMU*	9. *CMI*	17. *NSR*	25. *CMT*
2. *MSS*	10. *DMU-DMI*	18. *CBR*	26. *NMT*
3. *CMT*	11. *NMC*	19. *NVR*	27. *CMS*
4. *DMT*	12. *DSS*	20. *CSS*	28. *EMI*
5. *CBS-CMS*	13. *DMT*	21. *MMS*	29. *MSI*
6. *NST*	14. *NSI*	22. *CVS-MVS*	30. *NVT*
7. *CBT*	15. *EAS*	23. *CMU-CMS*	31. *MVU*
8. *EVI-EVS*	16. *CMR*	24. *DMU*	32. *NST-CST*

33. *DMI-DBI*	35. *CMI-CBI*	37. *CSU*	39. *DSU*
34. *CVU*	36. *CVS*	38. *EMU*	40. *NBI-EBI*

SUGGESTED READINGS

For readers who would like to go more deeply into the subject of the *Structure of Intellect* and its implications for psychology, the recommended source is:

Guilford, J. P. *The nature of human intelligence.* NYC: McGraw-Hill, 1967.

For those who would like information on the research background of the model, the source is:

Guilford, J. P. & Hoepfner, R. *The analysis of intelligence.* NYC: McGraw-Hill, 1971.

CHAPTER TEN

Problem Solving and Creative Thinking

In the preceding chapters you have seen a systematic parade of basic intellectual abilities, each illustrated by a task or two that emphasize it. This should not have left you with the impression, however, that in daily life each ability functions all by itself, and that all tasks can be classified each clearly with only one *SI* ability; far from it. The abilities do work together, but of course not all of them in any one activity. It is much easier to find tasks that call upon two or only a few abilities than tasks each of which involves only one ability. That is why it has been so difficult to discover what the different abilities are, and why it has required a method like factor analysis to tease them out of ongoing mental events.

Now that you have seen what most of the abilities are, and how they can operate in relative isolation, we should consider how they work together in some of the more complex operations in daily life. The *SI* model is a taxonomy. It tells us *which components* exist; components of mental functioning. The best place to see how these components work together is in problem solving and creative thinking. That is what this chapter is about. These two activities are well treated together because of their close relationship.

RELATIONS BETWEEN PROBLEM SOLVING AND CREATIVE THINKING

What is Problem Solving?

You encounter a problem whenever you face a situation with which you are not fully prepared to deal; you are not immediately ready to respond. Incidentally, the many "problems" that have been presented as illustrations in earlier chapters are not problems in a psychological sense to those who know the answers. When there is need to go beyond the items of information that we have already structured, there is a problem; there is need for new intellectual activity.

From this point of view, intelligence is readiness to solve problems. It is now clear that, beginning with Binet, the IQ testers were shunted in another direction. They tested for comprehension or understanding rather than for productive thinking, which is of greater importance in problem solving.

Education has tended to go in the same direction. Some years ago psychologists at the University of Illinois went into classrooms to tape record all that was said by teachers and pupils. They later estimated what proportion of the time the conversations dealt with each of the *SI* operations. As one could predict, a large proportion of the time was devoted to cognition and memory, with only a small percentage given to productive thinking. Problem solving does involve some cognition and memory exercises, but production and evaluation exercises are also needed.

What is Creative Thinking?

Creative thinking at its best leads to tangible products, such as a plan, a story, a poem, a painting, a musical composition, an invention, or a scientific theory. But most creative thinking is of a more common, home-grown variety, without any distinguished product. The activity may not even emerge in a visible product at all. Some of those who define creative thinking demand not only that there be a product but also that the product be novel in the population as well as socially useful.

From a scientific, psychological point of view, these requirements go too far. A science does not deal with social values; it only observes and reports, with resulting reflections and conclusions. It does regard novelty as a key characteristic of creative thinking, but restricts this feature to the thinker's own mental life; the creative idea is one that the thinker never had before; it is new to that person. We could never determine whether an idea is entirely new in the whole population. We stand a much better chance of showing that it is new to the individual. In order to distinguish creative thinking from ordinary learning, let us say that the creative idea comes from productive thinking in the *SI* sense.

Thus, it is possible to define creative thinking in a more definite way, by reference to the *Structure of Intellect*. As mentioned in the preceding chapters, the *SI* abilities most relevant to creative thinking come in the operation category of divergent production and the product category of transformation. Without either or both of these features being involved in the thinking episode, we cannot say that creative thinking has taken place. These abilities make essential contributions. They are the sources of novel ideas. This is not to say that other operations and other products do not make their contributions, for they do. But their roles are secondary and their appearances in the activity are incidental.

Creative Thinking in Problem Solving

At the beginning of this chapter it was stated that problem solving and creative thinking are closely related. The very definitions of those two activities show logical connections. Creative thinking produces novel outcomes, and problem solving involves producing a new response to a new situation, which is a novel outcome. Thus, we can say that problem solving has creative aspects.

We cannot so readily say that all creative thinking involves problem solving. In this connection we think of all the arts and we hesitate to make the second generalization. Superficially, at least, it does not appear that artists are solving problems in what they do. If we broaden our conception of problem solving, however, there is some support for this view. We could say that the artist's problem is one of self-expression. He has something that he wants to tell the world, or he wants to make tangible something that he thinks or feels. The origin of such a problem is within the artist himself.

Steps in Problem Solving and Creative Thinking

Similarities between creative thinking and problem solving are further shown by writers who have attempted to describe the major steps in either process. They have typically considered only cases that require some length of time to arrive at the final product or conclusion.

The American philosopher John Dewey concluded that a complete episode of problem solving includes the following steps, in order: (1) a difficulty is felt; (2) the difficulty is located and defined; (3) possible solutions are suggested; (4) consequences of those solutions are considered; and (5) a solution is accepted.

After considering the ways in which some historical creative people have done their work, Graham Wallas came out with the following list: (1) preparation (information is gathered); (2) incubation (information is allowed to simmer or ripen); (3) illumination (solutions emerge); and (4) verification (solutions are tested and elaborated). Wallas studied mostly writers and scientists.

Joseph Rossman studied only inventors and came out with a list very similar to Dewey's: (1) a need or difficulty is observed; (2) the problem is formulated; (3) available information is surveyed; (4) solutions are critically examined; (5) new ideas are formulated; and (6) new ideas are tested and accepted.

In general, we see many parallels between these three lists of steps. Investigations of how students tackle problems in the psychological laboratory verify the kinds of steps mentioned, but they show that the order of events is not strictly followed. There is frequent backtracking or returning to earlier steps when the going becomes difficult or rejections of ideas occur. Only Rossman's list makes any mention of this possibility.

A STRUCTURE-OF-INTELLECT PROBLEM-SOLVING MODEL

From time to time in this volume, connections were pointed out between certain SI abilities and both problem solving and creative thinking. We shall now bring all these relations together and put them in the form of a system in a *Structure-of-Intellect Problem-Solving* model, or *SIPS* model. It is an information-processing model, with events spread out in time, from start to finish of a problem-solving episode (see *Figure 10.1.*).

Underlying everything is the memory store, which contributes to everything that goes on. It also keeps a running record of what goes on, if that information is properly stored. The SI operations are represented by rectangles, with the exception of the operation of memory, which is indicated by arrows pointing into the memory store.

Events in problem solving begin with an input into the communication system, from the environment (E) and from the soma (S). The latter includes the body parts, hence it could take care of feelings and emotions that may instigate problem solving in producers of art in any of its forms.

Input of nerve-conducted information from the environment passes through a filtering process. A lower part of the brain (the reticular formation) serves as a gate, not permitting all incoming information to proceed to the higher, cortical, brain centers. This selective activity is the process of attention, which does not concern us here, except to know that certain biases and preconceptions, retained in memory storage, may prevent us from becoming aware of certain problems.

Nervous information that does get through the gate instigates the operation of cognition. This step includes two important events — awareness that a problem exists and comprehension of the nature of the problem. Suppose you are driving your car along the street and it suddenly stops. You know you have a problem. Diagnosing the problem takes further steps of cognition. You seek further information from the environment; some new input. You do some checking to see whether there is gasoline in the tank and also to see whether the electrical system is functioning. As you find these conditions apparently satisfactory, your

Figure 10.1

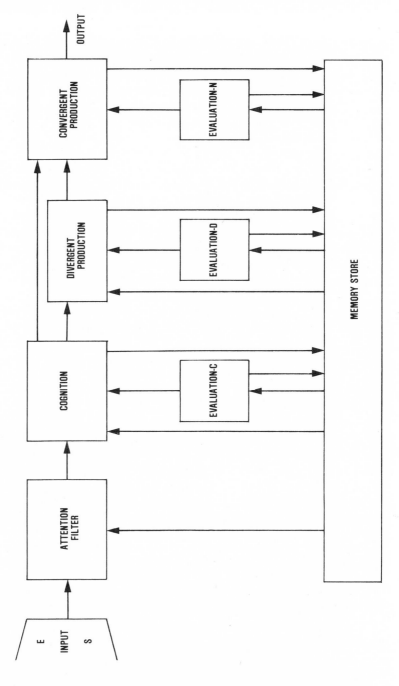

problem next is to obtain specialized help.

You are now at a solution-generation phase, and you think of one possible source of help after another, in divergent production. In this step you search your memory store, and you soon arrive at the idea that you are a member of the Auto Club. If you had thought immediately of the Auto Club without the broader search, you would have been engaging in convergent production, bypassing divergent production.

The fact that you may reject ideas anywhere along the way means that the operation of evaluation is functioning, as shown by the arrows leading upward from the evaluation rectangles in the model. Most retrieved items must run the gauntlet of evaluation, but in the case of divergent production some retrieved items escape evaluation by bypassing that operation. This kind of retrieval occurs with what is known as "suspended judgment," which Alex F. Osborn recommended as a very important tactic in creative thinking. Applying evaluation while engaged in divergent production can put a damper on retrieval of information from storage. Possibly very useful ideas could thus be nipped in the bud.

Sometimes we fail to solve a problem because we have not cognized it properly. We stubbornly attempt to solve the wrong problem. This outcome requires our taking a new look at the difficulty. Thus there is often some backtracking to earlier stages of the entire problem-solving process. We may even go back to the environment for additional fact finding. Following a new structuring of the problem is a new search for solutions in a new round of productive-thinking operations. There may be more than two such cycles before the goal is reached.

In the model, all the arrows pointing down to the memory store indicate that the various steps that we take are put into storage, for at least short-term memory, as a record of what we have done. Otherwise, we might be doomed to committing the same errors over and over.

If it is asked where creative activity occurs in the *SIPS* model, the most obvious answer is that it takes place wherever divergent production occurs. Although the most obvious place for this to happen is in the generation of possible solutions, it can also play a role in structuring the problem. We might say that structuring the problem is itself a kind of problem, and we thus have problems within problems.

Activities in the model are also creative where transformations occur. From the *SI* model, we have seen that transformations can happen in connection with any of the operations, including convergent production. The following illustration shows how transformations can play roles in structuring a problem.

In a certain organization, dissatisfaction developed with the financial information that was provided. The first thought was that the accounting system was in need of revision. But further investigation revealed that it was a personnel problem; a problem of lack of communication among certain key individuals. It was a behavioral problem rather than a semantic or symbolic one. This transformation came at the cognition stage in the *SIPS* model.

More obviously, transformations play roles at the production stage. We are frequently faced with the need of finding an object that will serve some unusual purpose; a redefinition is required. For example, we need to start a fire and no match or cigarette lighter is at hand. The sun is shining, so it occurs to us to use a pocket magnifying glass as a condensing lens to focus the sun's rays to start the fire. A reading glass is transformed into a fire starter.

THINGS THAT HELP OR HINDER CREATIVE THINKING

Thus far, we have been concerned with the psychology of creative thinking, anchored as it is in the *Structure of Intellect*. For the remainder of this chapter we shall consider ways in which you may control and improve your skills in problem solving and creative thinking. It is one thing to know what abilities we have, and this in itself is of use. There is more to be learned on where and how to use those abilities to advantage. There are strategies and tactics to be learned. There are favorable conditions to be applied and unfavorable conditions to be avoided or eliminated. We can exert some control over some of the conditions but not over others, as the following survey will show.

Environment

An individual would have greater chances of becoming outstandingly creative if he were born in the country rather than in a city. Alex F. Osborn has reported that an examination of *Who's Who* showed that an unusual proportion of those so recognized were born in the country. The same was true of a survey of distinguished scientists. Osborn goes so far as to say that "Urbanitis kills creativity," in his book *Applied Imagination.*

E. Paul Torrance has examined this problem in the case of children. He gave them an exercise on completing a story about a flying monkey. Children from the rural areas were more likely to let the monkey keep his wings, while those from the cities tended to make the monkey lose his wings, becoming more normal and less fanciful, before they were through.

As to family environment, it is found that the more creative scientists, and others, often came from unhappy homes, sometimes with wretched childhoods. There was often lack of parental harmony, of closeness with a parent, or there was a death of a parent. The most creative individuals were likely to be the first-born, or among the early children in the family.

Considering all these environmental conditions, a single hypothesis might be that the hard-luck or older child in the family faces an unusual number of problems to be solved, which gives him occasions for developing problem-solving skills. Urban life is more highly regulated than rural life, and the child does not face certain kinds of problems. He probably does have more interpersonal problems, however, which might prepare him better for creativity in the behavioral realm, such as politics or business. He does have certain advantages in his greater exposure to creative works of art and to technological products, but this may not be sufficient to offset limitations in the practice of handling his own problems.

Motivation

A person may have high status in some of the *SI* abilities most relevant for creative production, yet, without motivation to use those abilities, creative output may be very slight. The highly creative person must be driven with curiosity, and with this attitude he is more sensitive to problems. He must feel the challenge to solve problems and be persistent in his efforts to solve them. Many people who make creative production of some kind their life work would probably tell you that creative thinking is hard work. It is not always just a matter of having dreams. It is known that productive, creative people often observe regular work schedules and sometimes deadlines for certain pieces of work. Self discipline is often in control.

When you ask, "Why do they do it?" the answer is that they thoroughly enjoy it, in spite of the hard work. In his study of inventors, Rossman found that the leading source of satisfaction was often intrinsic to solving the problem itself. In fact, some inventors had hardly solved one problem when they immediately looked for another one, in order again to achieve that feeling of mastery, the satisfaction that can be gained from solving problems.

The Store of Information

In discussing productive-thinking abilities in earlier chapters it was emphasized that success in thinking depends in part upon the extent of pertinent information in the memory store. Outstandingly creative people generally agree that a good supply of information is necessary. This is because almost all the ideas we generate come by way of retrieval from our memory stores. As John Dewey put it, "We can have facts without thinking but we cannot have thinking without facts."

The strong drive of curiosity that was mentioned earlier strongly favors the accumulation of information to put into storage. A child is naturally curious, if he is healthy, for he has so much to learn. If his efforts to learn are rewarded he continues his investigations. If he is too often frustrated or even punished for his efforts, he tends to lose the habit of seeking information. We shall see later that curiosity makes another kind of contribution to problem solving.

Flexibility versus Rigidity

The creative person must be flexible; not rigid. We have seen before that there are at least two kinds of flexibility involved in productive thinking. One has to do with a ready shifting from class to class, as in the case of ability *DMC* (divergent production of semantic classes). Some people suffer from what might be called a disease of "hardening of the categories." Having put an object in a certain class, that is where such a person keeps it. You may recall that in thinking of alternative ideas, a class is a very common cue or instigator for retrieval of information from storage. We often recognize problems as belonging to classes. If we put the problem in the wrong class we are doomed to failure. Only by being ready to shift classes, in this case, can we proceed in the right direction. An example was cited earlier in which what was thought to be an accounting problem was actually a communication problem.

Another major kind of flexibility is concerned with transformations. A condition that prevents a needed transformation is illustrated by a story told by Sidney J. Parnes. A psychiatrist's patient insisted that he (the patient) was dead. In an attempt to rid the man of that mistaken belief, the doctor asked, "Do dead men bleed?" to which the man responded, "No." The doctor then pricked the man's finger, drawing a big drop of blood. Instead of being impressed with the fact that he was therefore alive, thus making the proper transformation, the man said, "Well, I'll be darned; dead men do bleed." Very few people have such paranoid delusions, but they do get tied up with other kinds of blocks to changes of views, in other words, blocks to transformations.

Group Thinking

Mainly at the *SIPS* step of production, but applying at other places as well, group problem solving is sometimes undertaken. This is a common objective of committee meetings. It is expected that different views of the problem will be brought out, so that, for one thing, the problem will be better defined. At the production phase, because memory stores of different individuals are likely to extend in somewhat different directions, the pool of alternative solutions should be considerably broadened. What one person does not think of another may. There is also interstimulation within the group, so that an idea that one person proposes instigates an idea in another, and one person can suggest improvements on another's idea. There is also the social-psychological phenomenon of "social facilitation," which means that people who see others performing the same task will work faster and better. This is not to be confused with motivation from rivalry, which can also contribute to motivation.

Group thinking also has some disadvantages. One is that there may be a certain individual who dominates the situation, whose views tend to channel the thinking of others, thus counteracting the opportunities for using a broader base of information. It is also known that individuals with higher levels of creative talent are likely to be individualists. They would probably prefer to work alone and would do their best work alone. Furthermore, on certain kinds of problems, at least, it has been found that individual workers are sometimes more productive than group workers.

Torrance has found that group problem solving works best when children are of similar IQ level or similar level in divergent-production abilities. These conditions give more of an equal chance to everyone to make contributions. With adult groups it is best not to include one who is in authority over others, or one who could make decisions affecting their welfare. There will be further thoughts on group problem solving later.

Criticism

Criticism of output from productive thinking seems to be inhibiting at almost any age. Children who have had criticism during an idea-generating session show reduced output as a consequence, even when criticism has been constructive. The probable reason in the latter case is that the child's attention is called to the need for criticism, which he then imposes upon himself in further creative efforts. In group problem solving, there is likely to be fear of being wrong and of being ridiculed.

If you have been in staff meetings, you are aware of some of the negative remarks that are too often made. These remarks may be intended to keep the other fellow from shining too brightly. They also have a depressing effect on the flow of ideas. Robert J. Gillespie, a distinguished inventor, has collected quite a list. Here are a few: *It won't work. — We've never done it before. — Let's shelve it for the time being. — The boss won't go for it. — Don't be ridiculous. — It's against our policy.* The best way to forestall such behavior is to have an understanding from the beginning of the session that everyone will apply the principle of suspended judgment, about which more will be said later.

Attitudes and Emotions

There are some special conditions, mostly self-imposed, that tend to suppress the flow of ideas. One of these conditions is a matter of taking sex roles too seriously. It has been commonly found that the more creative males, boys and men, in whatever area of creative production, tend to be a bit more feminine than others in their personality makeup. Also, the more creative women and girls tend to be a bit more masculine than their sex in general. Apparently, as society puts pressure on children to develop in the directions of stereotyped sex roles, their creative tendencies tend to suffer.

Too much attention to other norms may also provide handicaps. Pressure to be "normal" or "adjusted" according to generally accepted ideas of mental health may inhibit novel thinking. The highly creative child does stand out as being different, and he or she may not be able to face consequent disapprovals. Mankind, in general, seems unable to tolerate very much deviation from norms.

Various emotional states are said to be inimical to production of ideas; among them are prejudices, fear, anxiety, envy, negativism, apathy, and complacency. Also inhibiting are attitudes of respect for authority figures, attempts to please others in order to "get ahead," and lack of self confidence. Such conditions can be more or less controlled.

There has been a popular belief that a high level of creativeness is closely allied to madness. On listening to the rapid outpouring of ideas from a manic patient or the highly fanciful musings of a schizophrenic, one might gain such an impression. The trouble is, however, that such output is very lacking in relevance, a very important criterion for distinguishing psychotic output from normal output. In the former instance, that "computer between the ears" is out of order. There has also been some expectation to find that a highly creative person is neurotic. Psychological tests prove that the relationship is slightly in the opposite direction. A neurotic condition inhibits the flow of ideas.

STRATEGIES AND TACTICS

During past decades, certain people who have been concerned with problems in technology and industry, particularly, have developed some methods designed to promote increased effectiveness in problem solving, mostly without the benefit of a knowledge of the underlying psychology. Included are such workers as advertising writers, public-relations writers, engineers, and scientists working in industry. They have tried out different methods and have learned which ones work and which ones do not. We shall examine some of the successful methods and we shall find that they are usually based upon sound psychological principles. We begin with devices that apply along the course of flow of events in the *SIPS* model, then consider some more general ones.

If you should ask what you could do to be more sensitive to problems, one good answer is like that once given to a group of engineers who wanted to know how they could better bridge the gap between new scientific discoveries or technological advances, on the one hand, and adaptations of this information to uses in everyday life, on the other. This particular question arose during the early days of the country's space program, when new knowledge and new technical advances were already appearing to meet the demands of traveling and living in space and on the moon.

A possible answer to this question can take a cue from psychological tests, one of which was indeed called *Seeing Problems*. In this test, common objects are mentioned, and for each one the examinee is to list a number of difficulties that might occur in its normal uses. Analysis showed that all such tests represent *SI* ability *CMI* (cognition of semantic implications). An engineer could take one new discovery or gadget at a time, mull over its properties or attributes, what it can do or could be made to do, and list his ideas. Or he could go at the task from the other direction: He could start with some human need, perhaps having collected a large number of them as in a polling operation, then consider each need in connection with each of a number of things from the space program.

The person with curiosity is perpetually looking for implications. He examines and reflects upon every new thing he experiences. If they are man-made things he is likely to see deficiencies or difficulties in their use. A man notices that escalators travel across considerable space, so he sets for himself the problem of designing a circular escalator, after the model of the circular staircase. Another person notices how frequently a lawn has to be mowed, so he looks for a chemical that will retard its growth yet keep it green. Another person invents an artificial turf. Not so promising, however, is the effort to make hair on a wig grow so as to appear more natural.

Broaden the Problem

We are told that some persons who would like to solve a problem defeat themselves by narrowing the problem too soon. Instead of asking, "How can I build a better mousetrap?" one should ask, "How can we get

rid of mice?" This opens the gates to a broader search in perhaps more promising directions. Perhaps another method offers better
chances for improvement, or some entirely new method will result. Ask
not, "How can we build a better bus-transport system?" but, "How can
we move people more efficiently and attractively?" We might thus arrive
at some new mode of transportation, better than any now known.

Break the Problem into Sub-problems

This advice would seem to run counter to that just given, but
actually it does not. It can be applied after the broad problem is
conceived. It also applies to different situations. Suppose that in a
business organization the general problem is recognized as the need to
reduce costs. So stated the problem is too vague, for there are perhaps
30 places in the operations of the organization at which cost cutting
could be considered. After all places have been listed, there would be
much better preparation to work on each sub-problem.

None of this discussion precludes the fact that many very specific
problems come ready for solvers to think of solutions. In any case, we
need specific, well-defined problems to provide good cues for the step of
retrieval of information from the memory store. The clearer specifications make more certain the proper retrievals.

Ask Questions

A tactic that applies throughout the problem-solving episode is to
perpetually ask questions. This activity is, of course, the approach of
the person with curiosity. One can develop the habit of asking questions
—a habit that prods the brain into activity.

Certain questions are characteristic at different stages in problem
solving. In seeing problems, ask, "What is wrong or lacking?"; "What
more do we need?"; "What are the facts?"; "What other facts are
needed?"; "How are the facts interrelated?"; "Is the problem really
broader than that?"; and, "What are the part problems?"

At the time of generating ideas for solutions, ask, "What are the
requirements for a solution to this problem; what are its specifications?";
"What kind of ideas are needed?"; and again and again, "What else?"

In evaluating solutions, the questions would be, "What requirements must be satisfied?"; "What are the criteria of judgment?"; "Does
the solution satisfy the requirements?"

Suspended Judgment

The tactic of suspended judgment is an important aspect of the
brainstorming method. It calls for a complete separation in time of the

operations of production and evaluation. This principle is applied as shown in the *SIPS* model, where the retrieval process bypasses evaluation. Applying evaluation during the generating of ideas puts a damper on retrieval; ideas are often "headed off at the pass." During suspended judgment the quantity of ideas produced is markedly increased.

As Osborn maintained, quantity breeds quality. When more ideas are produced, the probability of a larger number of good ones is increased, provided the average quality does not deteriorate. As a matter of fact, it has been found that ideas produced later tend to be of higher quality than those that come more promptly.

Extended Effort

The effort to generate ideas should not be terminated too soon. The typical production rate is greatest immediately after the start, then it decreases as time goes on. You might produce ten ideas during the first minute, four during the next, and after eight minutes the rate might be less than one per minute. You might then think that you have exhausted your store of such items. After all, the memory store is not inexhaustible. But it is said that after you think you are through, you should ask, "What else?" and go on for ten more. Sidney J. Parnes found that the second half of the ideas produced contained 78 percent more good ideas than the first half. Thus, there is a principle that ideas tend to improve in value as time goes on. Alfred North Whitehead has been quoted as saying, "The 1000th idea may be the one that changes the world."

Attribute Listing

The previously mentioned technique of attribute listing has the effect of reclassifying things, which makes them more generally useful, and more applicable to unusual uses. To take a favorite example, the brick-uses task, mentioned in *Chapter 6*, will serve here. If, in listing uses for a common brick you break away from the common use as building material, your list can be greatly extended. A brick is relatively heavy for its size, hence could serve as paperweight or a doorstop. It is rectangular, hence could be used to draw straight lines, if need be. It is made of red or brown material, which could be ground up to make colored powder. It is hard and can be held in the hand, so it could be used as a hammer. It is porous and could therefore be used to filter water. If sufficiently rough it could be used as an abrasive, and so on.

There is a story about a young man who inherited from his father a brick-making factory. Bricks were not selling very well for their ordinary use as building material, so the young man had a "brainstorming" session with himself, thinking of other uses for bricks that might extend marketing possibilities. Whether he knew about the attribute-listing tactic or not, he was making use of it. It can often be used wittingly to advantage.

Forced Relationships

One possible way of obtaining novel ideas is to force two things into relationship where such a connection was not known before. Ask, "How can I relate X to Y?" At some time, someone did this to produce the wheelchair, the clock radio, and the amphibious landing craft. Sometimes this comes about because the problem calls for something with features that belong to two quite different objects. The person who is looking for a new hybrid plant has such a problem. It could happen that in just trying very hard to see a relation between two very different things, a relation comes that would lead to a useful product. One would then experience the unusual event of having a solution but looking for a problem!

Brainstorming

Probably the most widely employed strategy in problem solving is Osborn's famous brainstorming method. Ordinarily used in group thinking, it can also be used by individuals. According to the results of a survey by Torrance, brainstorming proved to be rather consistently the most effective method in improving problem-solving skills.

Several tactics are combined in a brainstorming session. Suspended judgment has been mentioned before. It is regarded as a most important feature, for without it there are likely to be inhibiting effects, such as from fear of appearing stupid or ridiculous, or the fear of criticism by others. Criticism of any kind is strictly taboo. "Free wheeling," which means letting yourself go, is encouraged; take your foot off the brakes. The emphasis is on quantity of ideas, with quality to be expected as a byproduct.

A number of other conditions are observed. The problem presented to the group by the leader should be specific, which implies that he has done groundwork prior to the session. However, this does not mean that there cannot be some sessions devoted to defining a problem. Follow-up sessions to the solution-finding phases are necessary also for the purpose of evaluation. By experience it has been found that the optimal size of the group is about a dozen, and a characteristic time period for the session is from 30 to 45 minutes.

Morphological Analysis

A special method, probably used more often in individual problem solving, is known as "morphological analysis." As an example of this procedure the *Structure-of-Intellect* model may be cited. A bit of history is that after some 40 intellectual abilities had become known through factor analysis, an attempt was made to organize them in some kind of system, for there were too many to remember easily. Various groupings could be made (classes) and various parallels (relations) were noticed. The three ways of classification became recognized as dimensions of the *SI* model — operations, contents, and products (see *Figure 9.1*). An important scientific value of the model has been to point to basic abilities still to be discovered, to fill vacant cells in the system as was done in completing the periodic table in chemistry. There are vacancies in the *SI* model still to be accounted for, which offer promising hypotheses for future investigation.

Engineer John E. Arnold has suggested how morphological thinking can be of great help to an inventor. Suppose an inventor were exploring the possibilities of creating some entirely new modes of transportation. He could think of all present ways of transporting people by considering first the major dimension of kinds of support for the vehicle — for example, solid ground, rail, water, air, oil, rollers, and perhaps others. Then he would consider sources of energy to propel the vehicle, excluding the muscle power of man or beast. The list would include: wind, gasoline, steam, electricity, to which could be added magnetism, gravity, jet stream, and atomic energy. The third dimension might be the position of the human body during travel, which would include, lying down, lounging, sitting, or standing, or combinations of these positions. A fourth dimension could be added if needed. As an interesting exercise for some readers, present modes of travel might be located within this three-dimensional matrix and then some vacant cells might be considered.

Myron S. Allen's book *Morphological Analysis* is devoted to this approach to creative thinking.

Try Incubation

In any idea-generating episode, even after the thinker has "tried for ten more ideas," there comes a time when it is only a practical matter to sign off from the proceedings. It would be more valuable, in fact, to let the matter rest for a time, but not to forget the problem. Most creative geniuses testify to the value of incubation, which means holding off actual work on a problem for a time, but keeping up the desire to solve it. The reward comes in the form of "inspiration," that is, sudden emergence of good ideas when not expected.

It is said that Edison made it a practice to have several different problems in the process of solutions during the same period of time, and that he switched from one problem to another whenever he got stalled. The "inspired" ideas have been reported to come at some very odd moments, such as while soaking in a bath tub, shaving, shining shoes, riding on a bus, or walking in the woods. One of the most common situations occurs in waking from a nap. You are advised to keep a pencil and note paper handy, just in case, for even some of the clearest ideas may vanish a short time later.

It is interesting to speculate that when you keep your desire to solve the problem, you really have not put it completely aside. In its retrieval activity, your brain keeps at the problem, and the very rare idea just happens to be out there on the low tail of your production curve. At any rate, it does not help to say that our unconscious minds are solving the problem for us. That is merely a figure of speech. Unless you have a dual personality, you have only one mind.

Altered States of Consciousness

Unusual states of consciousness were just mentioned as being favorable for retrieval of information during the period of incubation. This phenomenon has led some investigators to look further into the matter, and to try to induce similar favorable states. In modern history there have been reports of certain drug-induced states that were believed to facilitate creative thinking. But no drug state has seemed to hold up as being universally dependable. For a while, there was hope that the drug LSD (lysergic acid diethylamide) would be useful. During immediate aftereffects, the LSD user reports colorful hallucinations, which are, of course, his own inventions. Would repeated doses of LSD leave the person more generally creative? Experiments have failed to show any such benefits in the person's normal states. Such individuals are said to be left with a greater attention to sensations and greater aesthetic appreciation, but they are not generally better creative thinkers.

Because important creative discoveries have been made when the thinker is in a kind of dream-like state, efforts have been made to induce such conditions in various ways. Some approaches have been through Yoga, Zen meditation, Transcendental Meditation, and the like. Asiatic individuals who are highly practiced in such methods have not been noted for problem solving. Perhaps this is because they have not used the trance states for this purpose.

There is an interesting theory connected with the search for dream conditions in problem solving. Information in dreams is sensory or perceptual, mainly visual. This means it is right-hemisphere brain activity (in right-handed persons). One advantage of visual thinking over semantic thinking is its relative freedom from time limitations. Dreams take place within surprisingly short time intervals, whereas semantic (verbal) thinking is much slower, perhaps because it has been tied to speech. Visual thinking can also vividly illustrate some very complex things, for example, the *Structure-of-Intellect* model, or the *SIPS* model. These are shorthand expressions for many items of information. Such visual systems can be semanticized if need be, taking one item at a time.

In this connection, there is also the suggestion that young children are naturally creative in their imaginative, visual thinking. It is known that by the fourth grade or age of nine, children tend to lose something in creative thinking. Some of this is probably due to the increasing pressures from socializing processes. Perhaps it is also because that in the child's efforts to come to grips with reality he thinks more about what is and less about what could be. But possibly it is also because school work emphasizes verbal or semantic information, with some neglect of visual information. While the left brain hemisphere is being exercised the right hemisphere is neglected. The child gets out of the habit of thinking visually. These hypotheses need further investigation.

It is probable that at least one secret of the advantage of dream-like conditions for generating ideas is relaxation. It has been known for a long time that a good condition for retrieval of information from storage is a state of relaxation. When you have difficulty in recalling certain information and your desire to do so is very strong, this puts you in a tense condition, which is unfavorable. If you give up, at least temporarily, at some later moment when you are doing something else, the recalcitrant item pops into mind. The intervening relaxation from the effort to recall was probably the reason. The moral is that you have to learn to keep up your motivation to recall the item and at the same time just to wait passively for the idea to come.

In connection with favorable states for retrieval, we should note some of the more recent efforts to achieve relaxation through bio-feedback methods. During relaxation the brain is likely to be in a state in which the recorded brain-wave rhythms are in the alpha form, a slower, more regular pace. Efforts are made to train individuals to put themselves in the alpha-rhythm state. It is done by using a device that tells the person when his brain is in that condition by making a particular light or sound signal. The individual tries to make the signal appear.

Effects of this training upon creative thinking are largely yet to be determined.

Criteria of Evaluation

Most of the preceding space in this section has been devoted to the production of solutions to problems. It is time that the processes of evaluation received some attention. Actually there is not a great deal to say because evaluation has not been so extensively investigated.

According to the *SIPS* model, evaluation may occur all along the way in problem solving. But it is most conspicuous in connection with the production phase. At those points we have to decide whether the suggested solutions are correct or acceptable. Success in evaluation depends upon having the proper criteria with which to judge the solution. The criteria normally come from the known requirements, and the latter come from the conception of the problem. It is possible, however, that some new requirements may be introduced into the picture after the solutions have been generated.

The inventor Gillespie recommends the tactic of drawing up a checklist of requirements. To add to the list, some criteria outside the immediate problem may arise — for example, the effects of the solution on costs, on feasibility, and on public opinion. And, we might add, on ecology. Having a list of criteria, one should then give each of them a weight as to importance. It would then be possible to compare alternative solutions on the same basis. The task would be somewhat like that of judging products for prizes at a county fair.

INDUCING TRANSFORMATIONS

In discussions of strategies and tactics thus far, we have been concerned with improving production of ideas and comparatively little with the other main *SI* contributions to creative thinking by way of transformations. It is time to correct that imbalance.

Alex F. Osborn has left with us a checklist of tactics that are clearly aimed at inducing transformations. The items in his list actually name kinds of transformations such as occur in real objects. The list does not include all the kinds of transformations that occur in mathematics or in music, for example, but they go a long way.

Adapt

The main question here is, "What idea can I borrow from another source?" Modern composers have sometimes adapted melodies from the classics, with some changes. Designers of clothing have borrowed ideas from old-time costumes. From the idea of health insurance for humans comes the suggestion for health insurance for pets. Byproducts from factories have been utilized in making numerous secondary products that are useful and valuable. Some meat packers are said to use everything from the pig except its squeal. One manufacturer has gone into the production of brassieres for milk cows. The idea or object that is borrowed is, of course, not new, but its changed form is new.

Modify

In the process of modifying, we are striving to improve something, or to make an idea better than it is. Improvements in objects and in designs are so common that illustrations are numerous. Styles change, but usually very gradually, for people are evidently loathe to accept radical changes, as in the Edsel Ford or the postwar Studebaker, if you remember that far back. Putting music on delivery trucks for bread or ice cream in place of irritating horns or whistles was a welcome move. The change to an umbrella material that one can see through must have won the thanks of many a person in rainy climates.

Substitute

Questions applying here are: "What instead?"; "Who else?"; or "Where else?" and the like. Possibly no one knows how many substitutions were made in the material used in a light bulb since that day when Edison found that a carbon filament would work in a vacuum. Archimedes provided a history-making substitution. It has been said that he was asked to find out whether the king's crown contained as much gold as it was supposed to. He could weigh the crown, but measuring its volume presented a problem, until he thought of seeing how much water it would displace when immersed.

A recent important industrial substitution uses a very thin glass fiber in place of more expensive copper wire, as in telephone circuits. In another substitution, a computer receives confessions instead of a priest. The latter is by no means the end of substitutions involving computers, as in automation in industry.

Magnify

Can we add, multiply, or extend something to advantage? It is very often done. Increases can be in size, strength, time, or frequency of occurrence. Sales of products have increased on offering premiums or adding coupons. A cook shows creativity by adding ingredients to a recipe. New features have been continually added to motor cars, television sets, and other products. We are attracted to purchases that offer "double your money back," and to propositions that offer "killing two birds with one stone."

Minify

Can we gain something by making a product smaller, or by omitting something, or dividing it? There are definite advantages in having some things made small — watches, radios, and motor cars, for example.

Someone has recently printed X-ray pictures on 3 × 7 cards for storage purposes, where they were formerly 14 × 17 inches. Foods have been condensed or reduced to powder through dehydration. Cooking times have been cut in fractions by freezing foods, and by using pressure cookers and microwave ovens. Some things have lost disposable parts by omission, as the tubeless tire and the stringless "string" bean. The marketing of chickens and turkeys has been better adapted to small families by cutting them up and selling separate parts.

Rearrange

Can we gain by revising the order of things? It might be a case of room arrangements of a house we are planning to build or the reshuffling of furniture within a room, in order to obtain a more usable and attractive effect. A revision of events in a schedule may be to the advantage of several people. It is said that cafeterias have found that more desserts are sold when they are placed first in the food line.

Reverse Things

Will it help to turn things completely around? This, of course, is a special, extreme case of rearrangement. In these days of women's lib one might think of writing a story in which the boss is a woman and the secretary is a man. Sometimes mechanical devices have been improved by turning something end for end, upside down, or inside out. The same principle may apply in construction operations.

Sidney X. Shore tells an interesting story that has a real twist. A certain Indian Chief saw that two of his tribesmen had horses, either of which he would like to have for himself. He told the men to engage in a race, and the horse that won would become the property of the Chief. Someone had the courage to remind the Chief that neither man would try to win the race, "Ah ha," said the Chief, "you have not heard my other condition. Each man will ride the other's horse."

Combine

This kind of creative step is so commonplace among productive operations that it hardly needs mentioning. Some examples may be helpful, however. Going back in history, we note that Benjamin Franklin invented the bifocal lens for spectacles. The trifocal lens was more recently introduced. The wooden pencil was first made without an eraser attached, and someone later thought of putting them together. In more modern times advances in industry have depended upon the invention of alloys and on products from synthetic chemistry. A recent important innovation has been the fusing of glass with metal.

To take an example closer to home, consider a problem that you may have known about. It probably arises only in more rural areas. How can you prevent the neighbor's chickens from coming over and ruining your garden? You do not want to spend money to build a wall or fence, and you do not want to take your neighbor into court.

This problem calls for the invention of a plan — a semantic system. One person's proposed solution was as follows. He would soak kernels of corn in alcohol over night, and scatter some of them about the garden the next morning. The chickens would come over and gorge themselves with the impregnated corn. In due time, they would become groggy and fall over in a stupor. He would then toss the chickens over in the neighbor's yard, apparently dead. They would probably survive the spree and the neighbor would hopefully get the point.

More Generally

Checklists such as Osborn's could be drawn up for encouraging transformations in other areas of creative production. Some tactics would probably overlap those already given, but some would be unique to their areas.

TRAINING FOR CREATIVE THINKING

With so many procedures designed to help in problem solving and creative thinking, as described in the pages of this book, the prospects would seem to be good for improving the skills of individuals in these operations. The methods can clearly be taught, and that is being done on an increasing scale. There were only a few courses on the subject in the 1930's, but since that time there are said to have been hundreds. The great majority of them have been in industry, such as General Electric and AC Sparkplug Corporations, and in some governmental departments such as the Department of Defense, but curiously still very few in educational institutions.

Clearly a prime mover in promoting instruction in creative thinking and problem solving has been Alex F. Osborn, through his book,

Applied Imagination. In 1955 he initiated the *Annual Creative Problem-Solving Institute* at the University of Buffalo.

The preceding year he organized the *Creative Education Foundation,* in order to bring about a more creative trend in education, government, and industry. Through the implementation of its own teachings, the *Foundation* has been able to maintain its ambitious efforts and services: cosponsorship of graduate and undergraduate courses; annual *Creative Problem-Solving Institutes;* dissemination of pertinent printed and audio-visual material; publication of the quarterly *Journal of Creative Behavior;* and also research in the nature and nurture of creative behavior. Its accomplishments have received worldwide recognition.

Both the *Institute* and the *Foundation's* momentum are capably being carried forward by Sidney J. Parnes and his associates at the State University College at Buffalo campus. Parnes heads the Department of Creative Studies, which, among other things, offers instruction through a Master's degree in the field.

During the last two decades, a number of investigators have tested experimentally the extent to which instruction in creative thinking by different methods may contribute to improvement in personal status, particularly in abilities *DMU, DMC,* and *DMT.*[1] Almost always significant gains in performance were found, even with short periods of instruction. For example, Torrance found that children obtained increased scores in tests after only 20 minutes of instruction concerning the nature of divergent production.

The most extensive educational experiment of this kind was performed by Sidney J. Parnes and Ruth B. Noller at the State University College at Buffalo. A curriculum including four semester courses was planned. Entering freshmen were invited to take the curriculum as an elective, and more than 300 accepted. Of these, half were selected at random to take the course, the experimental group, and the others did not take the course but had agreed to serve as a control group. Psychological tests were administered to both groups at the beginning and at intervals during the two years, many of the tests being selected to represent *SI* abilities.

The results from the *SI* tests showed generally more gains for the experimental group than for the control group, not only in divergent-production abilities but also in cognition and convergent-production abilities. Evaluation abilities were not well sampled, and there was little reason to expect gains in memory abilities. As to content, gains were

---

[1]Full names of these abilities may be found in *Chapter 6* or see *Figure 9.1.*

mostly in semantic and behavioral areas, with none in symbolic abilities.

There was other evidence of gains in the trained group. They were much superior to the untrained group in planning in a given research problem. They reported that they were helped in other courses and felt more able to enter into class discussions. They felt more able to cope with problems in general.

Increased self-confidence seems to be a common result of such training. In a county-wide experiment in Polk County, Iowa, children were given exercises in creative thinking. One of the most notable changes reported in the children, as derived from a psychological test, was a gain in self-respect, particularly among the black children.

It can be emphasized that along with the teaching of methods and the application of exercises, there should also be some presentation of theory, as much as the learner can comprehend. G. A. Forehand and W. J. Libby, Jr. did a study at the University of Chicago in teaching government administrators to think creatively. One group was given exercises only while the other had exercises plus theory. Those who had had the theory later showed the effects in their jobs by suggesting more innovative ideas. Torrance's experiments (referred to earlier) also verify the positive effects of instruction in this area.

EDUCATION OF THE INTELLECT IN GENERAL

The evidence just cited regarding improvements in creative-thinking skills and the abilities underlying them shine a light of optimism on future endeavors to elevate abilities. As stated at the very beginning of this book, what the world needs now is many more able problem solvers. It was pointed out that failure to solve problems leads to frustrations, and frustration leads to aggression, violence, and war. Those in the field of education should make an all-out effort to prepare children and young people to solve problems. As shown by the *SIPS* model, problem solving involves a very large number of the basic intellectual abilities.

Development of Abilities

Evidence has just been cited to show that certain *SI* abilities can be strengthened by exercise and by instruction as to their natures. The inference is that this finding will be more general when the needed experiments have been done. Heredity may set upper bounds upon development of each ability in an individual, but probably very rarely does anyone push his development to his limits.

It is said that individual differences in IQ are 60 to 80 percent determined by heredity. But even that situation leaves much room for the effects of environment, including education. It is a well-demonstrated fact that as the average educational level of a society increases, the average IQ also rises. Also to be considered is the fact that the IQ represents only a small proportion of the *SI* abilities. We cannot assume that the percentage of hereditary determination cited above applies also to the great remainder of intelligence. On the other hand, we know that some abilities can be strengthened by training. This should encourage us to try for gains more generally.

The Structure of Intellect in Education

The implications of the *Structure of Intellect* in education are so numerous that it is impossible to do more than list the major ones here. Certain consequences should follow in the philosophy of education, in curriculum building, and in teaching and assessment practices. One objective of education should always be to promote intellectual development. From the *SI* view of intelligence, we not only see what has to be done to approach that objective but there is new evidence that we can do so.

As we survey the educational scene with the *SI* model as our frame of reference, we can see several instances of imbalance in present operations. The serious neglect of the productive-thinking abilities and the relative overemphasis on cognition and memory was mentioned earlier. We now have a better basis for seeing that it is not enough to fill young heads with knowledge, although this is a necessary step; we must give the students instruction and exercise in using that knowledge. The knowledge should be made functional.

Any suggestion for achieving better balance with respect to kinds of informational content is debatable. But it would seem desirable to see that each child gains adequate acquaintance with all kinds of content, for lines of interest seem to run parallel with kinds of content. Some students like to deal with concrete things, which involve figural or perceived information. Some like symbolic information, so should be expected to be attracted to mathematics and perhaps to foreign languages. Others enjoy more their dealings with verbalized ideas — semantic information. Still others are more interested in people; their attention is drawn by behavioral information. Kinds of occupations can also be roughly classified along the same lines, as was pointed out in *Chapter 2*.

There are probably also some imbalances among the teaching operations, with respect to products of information, as there obviously has been among the kinds of tests in IQ scales. In the latter, units and systems receive the most attention and classes the least. From what has been said in this chapter, it should be clear that not only classes but also relations, implications, and transformations are very important. Teachers who have tried to use *SI* concepts in their teaching have reported that they find the product categories to be the most useful. Actually teaching children as much as they can understand regarding the products has been reported to be helpful.

An educational institution that wants to keep its fingers on the pulse of intellectual development of its children would find it advantageous to assess them with respect to *SI* abilities. A child's intellectual status would then be expressed in terms of a profile of scores rather than a single IQ value. Differential assessment is of greatest value in connection with diagnosis of cases with learning difficulties in slow learners. Points of weakness can thus be located and special treatment can be prescribed.

Mary N. Meeker, of Loyola and Marymount University of Los Angeles, has probably done most to apply *SI* concepts to remedial education, as well as to educational problems in general. She has not only developed new *SI* tests for children but also workbooks of exercises for different *SI* abilities. She has founded the *SOI* Institute, for fostering the use of *SI* in education.

In Japan, a Learned Society for Intelligence Education is doing much to promote development of *SI* abilities in many schools, starting at the kindergarten level.

If, through education, we can produce populations of creative problem solvers, we shall have done much to ease world tensions and to make men and women happier creatures.

SUMMARY

In problem solving and creative thinking we find intellectual abilities working together, if the problem and its solution are at all complex. The two kinds of exercise are intimately related, for the solving of a problem calls for novel steps in behavior, and this means creative performance.

Because of similarities of the steps in all kinds of problem-solving episodes, it is possible to think of a basic model representing the common mental events taking place therein. The *SIPS (Structure-of-Intellect Problem-Solving)* model is such a system. Somewhere in the model, all of the *SI* operations are found, and different kinds of items of information are involved, depending upon the nature of the problem.

Briefly, the first event is awareness that a problem exists (cognition of implications). The problem is structured or understood, with specified needs for certain kinds of items of information in order to begin solving it (cognition of relations and systems). Ideas for solutions occur to the problem solver (divergent and convergent production). Both the conception of the problem and the suggested solutions are judged to be good or bad (evaluation). The flow of information is possibly put into storage for later use, immediate or delayed (memory).

Because of the important role of creative thinking, not only in problem solving, as in science and technology as well as in personal affairs generally, but also in the arts, considerable attention has been given to things that should make the individual more creative. Besides advantages coming from strength in certain *SI* abilities, there are traits of motivation and temperament to be considered, as well as favorable and unfavorable environmental conditions.

Successful efforts are being made to improve creative-thinking skills of individuals, through exercises of various kinds and instruction regarding the nature of creative thinking. Quite a number of special tactics have been designed to aid the problem solver.

Of broader scope are some current efforts to apply knowledge of the *SI* abilities quite generally in education — in planning curriculum, in lesson plans, and in classroom teaching and testing. The outcome could be a population of skilled problem solvers, not only in science, technology, and art, but also in human relations, where problems are most vital.

SUGGESTED READINGS

Readers who would like to pursue these subjects further may find the following books of value:

Biondi, A. M. *Have an affair with your mind.* Great Neck, NY: Creative Synergetics Associates, Ltd., 1974.

Crawford, R. P. *The techniques of creative thinking.* Wells, VT: Fraser, 1964.

Getzels, J. W. & Jackson, P. W. *Creativity and intelligence: explorations with gifted students.* NYC: Wiley, 1962.

Guilford J. P. *The nature of human intelligence.* NYC: McGraw-Hill, 1967.

Guilford, J. P. *Intelligence, creativity, and their educational implications.* San Diego, CA: Knapp, 1968.

Meeker, M. N. *The structure of intellect: its interpretations and uses.* Columbus, OH: Charles E. Merrill, 1969.

Osborn, A. F. *Applied imagination.* (3rd ed.) NYC: Scribner, 1963.

Parnes, S. J. & Harding, H. F. (eds.). *A source book for creative thinking.* NYC: Scribner, 1962.

Taylor, I. A. & Getzels, J. W. (eds.). *Perspectives in creativity.* Chicago: Aldine, 1975.

Torrance, E. P. *Guiding creative talent.* Englewood Cliffs, NJ: Prentice-Hall, 1962.

Index

Notes

Notes